JANE FONDA

JANE FONDA

AN AMERICAN ORIGINAL

TOM COLLINS

Franklin Watts ☆ 1990
New York ☆ London ☆ Toronto ☆ Sydney

Photographs courtesy of: Author's collection: 5, 10 top;
Fonda collection: 1, 3, 6, 7, 8, 9, 10 bottom, 11, 12, 13, 15;
Fonda Films: 14 top, 14 bottom and 16 (Harry Langdon);
Omaha Community Playhouse (John Savage): 2, 4

Library of Congress Cataloging-in-Publication Data

Collins, Tom, 1946–
Jane Fonda, an American original / by Tom Collins.
p.   cm.
Includes bibliographical references (p.   )
Summary: A biography of the controversial, talented, and many-
faceted Jane Fonda.
ISBN 0–531–15149–2—ISBN 0–531–10929–1 (lib. bdg.)
1. Fonda, Jane, 1937–   —Juvenile literature. 2. Motion picture
actors and actresses—United States—Biography—Juvenile literature.
[1. Fonda, Jane, 1937–   . 2. Actors and actresses.] I. Title
PN2287.F56C6   1990
791.43′028′092—dc20
[B]
[92]   89–25100   CIP   AC

Dedicated to
Ella Evelyn Irish Brackett
with Love and Affection
and Because She Raised
Such a Lovely Daughter

Acknowledgments

The author wishes to thank Jeanne Vestal, Judie Mills, and Mary Perrotta for their hard work on this book, and especially Margie Leather, a paragon of patience and support under stress. Nancy Garden, an editor's editor, improved the manuscript immeasurably by her brilliant review, equally sensitive and meticulous, which was a revelation. Steve Rivers was consistently helpful with details large and small. Finally, Jane Fonda's kindness and courtesy have been more appreciated than it is possible to say.

CONTENTS

1

A ROTTEN SUMMER

Jane Fonda stood at the end of the diving board and looked at the icy mountain lake below. Shivering a little in the cool breeze, she took a deep breath, launched herself into the air, and descended with a mighty splash. Her teeth chattered as she climbed out of the water and prepared to try again.

Although she could easily let a stunt woman replace her for the back flip called for in the script, Jane was determined to master the trick herself. After all, she was working with Katharine Hepburn on this picture and wanted to make a good impression on the legendary actress.

Hepburn had been a competitive diver in her youth. Now in her seventies—almost twice as old as Jane—she could still do a back flip and made sure Jane knew it. Jane felt it would be especially embarrassing to fail, considering that she led morning exercises for the cast and crew each day and had opened her workout studio the year before. Responding to the challenge, she practiced every day with a coach until she had mastered the unfamiliar maneuver.

Then Hepburn asked her, "Don't you feel good?"

"Just terrific," Jane said, suddenly realizing it was true. She *was* proud of her accomplishment.

"Everybody should know that feeling of overcoming fear and mastering something," Hepburn told her. "People who aren't taught that become soggy!"

Telling the story later, Jane commented, "Katharine Hepburn is the least soggy person I know." That's a wonderful thing to have someone say about you—at any age. And no one can accuse Jane of being "soggy," either. The movie she was making, *On Golden Pond*, was for her own company. And it not only brought her sixth Academy Award nomination; it earned Oscars for her father, Henry, and for Hepburn.

For most people, the word *actress* calls up the image of a glamorous star, someone who wears beautiful clothes and mingles with other celebrities at lavish Hollywood parties. Anyone in "the business" knows that despite all the glitter, stars are hard workers who often have to get up before dawn to go to work and whose schedules are so hectic they may have little time for their families or themselves.

But not too many people in the business or outside it would say that most stars fight for political causes, write best-selling exercise books, run a children's camp, cook for their family, and go to their son's Little League games.

But Jane Fonda is a star who does all those things. She has also received two Oscars, an Emmy, and numerous other acting awards. She has had as many as three exercise videotapes on the industry's best-seller list at the same time and has written not just one but four best-selling books. *Jane Fonda's Workout*, an exercise book, was the most popular nonfiction volume in America for more than two years.

Her success as a performer, exercise authority, and businesswoman made her the fourth most admired woman in the country, according to a 1982 Gallup poll. The 1984 *World Almanac* called her the nation's third most influential woman. And in 1986, *U.S. News & World Report* found her the number-one hero for women eighteen to twenty-four years old. Both men and women in that age group voted her the woman they most admired.

Also much admired—and often condemned—for her political activities and her role in protesting the Vietnam War, Jane has had yet another career as the wife of California assemblyman Tom Hayden and as the mother of two children. She likes to cook, spend time at home with her family, and attend her son's Little League games. In the summer, she spends as much time as she can at the children's camp she and Tom started in the Santa Ynez Mountains above Santa Barbara.

Yet beneath this American success story there is another story that is very different. It is not easy to imagine how a beautiful and talented sex symbol became widely known in the late 1960s for her opposition to U.S. participation in the war in Vietnam. Even though that was more than twenty years ago, there is a small but outspoken minority for whom she will always be "Hanoi Jane," a symbol of all those who opposed that controversial war. This minority cannot forgive her—especially for being right—but at the same time, many others who also worked to try to stop that war consider her opposition nothing less than heroic.

To understand all the facets of Jane Fonda's complex personality, you must go back to the beginning. The first things you need to know about Jane Fonda are that her father was very famous, that she was born rich, and that her mother took her own life when Jane was twelve years old.

☆ ☆ ☆

"My only major influence was my father," Jane said once. And she didn't just mean that he was an actor and she had followed in his footsteps. She knew he was probably the most famous and respected actor in America—"a national monument," she once called him, asking, "How can you compete with that?"

Growing up in his shadow, she felt she couldn't just be "good enough"; she'd have to be the best. That's a tough challenge for anyone, in any field, but it was a particularly daunting prospect for Jane when she was a teenager because she felt fat, unattractive, insecure, and not very talented.

Some of this insecurity surely came from a lack of encouragement, but even worse was her father's coldness—his almost complete lack of ability to show affection even to the people he loved most. He could tell other people how proud he was of Jane, but he did not tell her. In March 1978, when Jane was in her forties and Henry was near the end of his life, she was amazed to hear him reveal on national television some feelings for her that she never knew he had. The event was the American Film Institute tribute in his honor, and what he said began with the story of his own start as a performer.

Born Henry Jaynes Fonda on May 16, 1905, he moved from Grand Island, Nebraska, to Omaha when he was six months old. At twenty, he got his start as an actor because his mother asked him to fill in at the Omaha Community Playhouse, which needed someone to fill a part. He was hooked. His first starring role came a year later, and his own father was so upset at Henry's undertaking of such a risky career that the two didn't speak for six weeks. But on opening night Henry received a standing ovation. Afterward, when the family was talking things over in the living room, someone ventured a tiny criticism. "Shut up!" said his father sharply. "He was perfect!"

Henry always claimed that was the best review he ever received, but this time that wasn't the end of the story. He went on to talk about Jane, the criticism she had received, and how he felt about her. "And if I ever heard anybody say anything about her," he added, "I'd say, 'Shut up. She's perfect!' " It caught her completely by surprise, and her throat seized up with emotion. "It just wiped me out," she said. She never expected him to say anything like that—and in all their years together, he never had.

"I really love him, but it's just that he doesn't tell *me*," she said. Especially when she was growing up, that was very hard to deal with. But what Jane had no trouble accepting was her father's intense personal commitment to liberal political causes.

"I was brought up to believe that if anyone in the world was in trouble—that is what my father believed—that we were all in trouble," Jane once explained. "If anyone is being harassed, if anyone's life is threatened, if there is discrimination against any of us, it is a concern for all of us."

Henry had campaigned for President Franklin Roosevelt, for example, and against Spain's Fascist dictator, Francisco Franco. Later, in a rage over Sen. Joseph McCarthy's anticommunism crusade, which he considered hypocritical, Henry kicked in a television set. When Jane was fourteen, he supported Adlai Stevenson's valiant but doomed bid for the presidency. It would seem inevitable that she would absorb these values and the rock-ribbed integrity with which her father supported them.

"My father wants things to be true, honest, real, and important," Jane said in 1965, several years before she plunged into political action. "I don't think I'm courageous enough." Like his professional success, she found his strong commitment to social justice a hard act to follow.

One of the most unforgettable moments in Henry's life occurred when he was about thirteen or fourteen. A young black man had been arrested for rape, and an angry crowd had been gathering in front of the town courthouse all afternoon. Henry's father worked at a printing plant nearby, and that night after supper they drove there and stood inside the darkened building, watching the mob go wild with a frenzy of hate and rage.

No charges had been filed, and there had been no trial, but the crowd wanted punishment. Men were cursing and screaming, eager to use the guns and clubs they had brought. When the mayor and sheriff failed to calm the crowd, a group went in and brought out the terrified prisoner. In his autobiography, years later, Henry vividly recalled what happened next:

A great huzzah went up when they saw the poor fellow. They took him, strung him up to the end of a lamppost, hung him, and while his feet were still dancing in the air, they riddled his body with bullets. It was the most horrendous sight I'd ever seen. Then they cut down the

*body, tied it to an auto, and dragged it through the
streets of Omaha.*

Henry's father never preached, never said a word. He just made
sure his son had seen everything before they drove home in
silence. And Henry never forgot. Jane learned about the incident
one day when she was a little girl and the two were in the car
together. Although she had never known any black people, she
had heard the word "nigger" and used it, not even really knowing what it meant. Henry turned around and slapped her and
then told Jane about the lynching he had seen, so that she would
never forget how ugly racism is.

Curiously, although Henry did not encourage Jane's tenta-
tive first steps into acting, they did appear together on the
Omaha stage where he had gotten his start and again in Cape
Cod at the same theater he had settled into after failing to find
work in New York. The troupe he joined had included Mildred
Natwick, Joshua Logan, and later, James Stewart—all of whom
would eventually become world famous. Also among the players
was actress Margaret Sullavan, who became Henry's wife on
Christmas Day, 1931. The marriage lasted less than a year, but
his career continued to pick up steam, especially after he moved
to Hollywood in 1935.

When James Stewart followed, the two rented a farmhouse
in Brentwood, near the present site of UCLA and not far from
the hilltop farmhouse where, soon after, Jane grew up. Their
next-door neighbor was Greta Garbo, a famous actress from
Sweden, and they double-dated Lucille Ball and Ginger Rogers,
who were also just starting out.

Henry was in England shooting that country's first Techni-
color movie, *Wings of the Morning*, when he met Frances
Seymour Brokaw, who would become his second wife—and
Jane's mother. Just twenty-six years old, she was a widow with a
large fortune and a four-year-old daughter, Frances de Villiers,
who was known as Pan.

When Henry finished filming, he and Frances went to Berlin for the Olympics and found the city filled with soldiers, uniforms, and swastikas. Soon the "twisted cross" of the Nazis would be on the move as Adolf Hitler, the German dictator, tried to conquer Europe. Sobered by what they had seen, the couple returned to the United States. They had a fashionable wedding in New York on September 16, 1936, and the next day the groom flew back to Hollywood to begin work on a new picture.

Frances soon joined him, and the couple settled into a little Brentwood house only two blocks from where Henry's first wife, actress Margaret Sullavan, was living with Leland Hayward, her new husband. Everything was cozy, since the women liked each other and Hayward was both Henry's agent and a good friend. Later, he became Henry's producer as well.

A year after the wedding, Frances flew back to New York to be with her obstetrician, and on December 21, 1937, Jane Seymour Fonda was born. She was named after the third wife of England's King Henry VIII, who was a distant relative of Frances, and after Henry's mother, whose maiden name was Jayne.

As the world drew closer to war, Henry turned out one major film after another, many revealing his strong sense of right and wrong. In *Blockade*, for example, made in 1938, he had a speech about the bombing of civilians in Spain that he would have cause to remember during the Vietnam era. "It's not war," insisted the character he played. "War's between soldiers. It's murder—murder of innocent people. There's no sense to it. The world can stop it. Where is the conscience of the world?"

The following year he played the title role in *Young Mr. Lincoln*, which established him firmly in the public mind as a remarkable actor. Somehow it seemed that Henry really *was* Lincoln, and it was easy for people to believe that he had the same personal qualities as the Illinois lawyer he had brought to life.

Then, on February 23, 1940, Peter Henry Fonda was born. It was just a month after *The Grapes of Wrath* opened—one of Henry's most important movies. Frances recovered more slowly from this birth. Henry flew back to California with his son, and Frances followed after she had recovered from what doctors suspected was a kidney problem.

With the success of one movie after another, the Fondas had saved enough money to build their dream house. For years they had wanted to buy hilltop property at 600 Tigertail Road in Brentwood, above Sunset Boulevard. It offered a 360-degree panoramic view, and even at $3,000 an acre, they thought the nine-acre parcel was worth the investment.

The couple knew just what they wanted to build—a Cape Cod–style house with oak beam ceilings, a wood-and-brick fireplace, window seats, and a little cupola with an old school bell in it to summon the children to dinner. A tennis court was carefully shaded from the wind, and a swimming pool was disguised as a farm lake.

There was also room for Henry to pursue his hobby (painting pictures), a garden shed, a playhouse, a cabana, and a small playground with a jungle gym to climb on. A separate building incorporated the garage and servants' quarters. There would be numerous servants—cooks, maids, gardeners, and nurses—while Jane was growing up. Pan, almost six years older than Jane, had a governess of her own and led a largely separate existence.

Before any building started, however, the landscaping was done. Henry and Jane flew kites to determine wind currents and carefully studied the patterns of light and shade. Trees were moved, gardens planted, flower beds laid out. When it was all done, the two-story house fronted on the road and had a wonderful view.

Jane's room, at the rear, looked north and west toward the peaks and rugged canyons of the Santa Monica Mountains.

From other windows they could see Los Angeles to the east and the Pacific Ocean to the southwest. Inside, many of the furnishings were colonial antiques. There were hooked rugs on the floor, built-in bookcases, and Jane's room had an old-fashioned four-poster bed. She and Peter also had carved merry-go-round horses to play on and a whole menagerie of dogs, cats, chickens, and other animals. Later on, there were even two burros that Jane fed and watered each morning.

But while the Fondas had been concentrating on their own affairs, the world situation had gotten worse. A few weeks before Jane's fourth birthday, the Japanese attacked Pearl Harbor, and the next day, December 8, 1941, the United States entered the war. The entire country united against its enemies, and soon everyone had sons, brothers, or friends fighting overseas. No one argued over which side was "the good guys," but what was not clear was whether the good guys were going to win. All anyone knew for sure was that there was no choice, or else the future would look (as George Orwell predicted in his famous book 1984) like "a boot stamping on a human face—forever."

After talking things over with his wife, Henry decided that he could not continue as usual while there was a war to be won. He wasn't crazy about getting hurt, but he said he would rather be in the newsreels than at the studios.

"I don't want to do any more movies," he told Frances. "I don't want to sell war bonds or be photographed with soldiers and sailors. I want to be a sailor." Henry finished the picture he was working on and the very next day, August 24, 1942, went down and enlisted in the navy. The family had hardly been in their new home for a year when he left, and it was three long years before Jane saw her father again. By then he had become a lieutenant, and she was almost eight years old.

"I remember the Second World War," Jane says. "I remember air raids. There were air raids where you had to put up black curtains over the windows at night so the light wouldn't show. I remember, before Dad went overseas, that my mother and father volunteered to go at night—I never knew quite where—to look at the sky. And I remember terrible fear.

"I remember when a submarine was sighted off the coast, my dreams were all about an invasion. It was a very real fear that we were going to be invaded. My father was gone for the whole first part of my life. All I knew about him was letters that would come from various battleships that he was on in the Pacific. It was a time of fear that our fathers were going to die overseas. And some of them did.

"And it was a time of tremendous national unity. We all pitched in. You know, we would have various collections at school. I remember victory gardens, where we grew vegetables to help avoid food shortages. Everybody participated. We had one at school. And everyone was united. That was my memory of it."

☆ ☆ ☆

Since Jane's brother, Peter, was younger than she, he often got much of their mother's attention, which meant that Jane sought out love and support from her father. There's no question that Henry loved his daughter, but he didn't always show that love in ways she could understand. He tended to be quiet, with long silences and stern, impatient ways like those of his own father.

In those days, the area where they lived had not yet been filled with shopping centers and housing developments. Jane and her best friend, Sue-Sally Jones, even went horseback riding together in woods that are now long gone. When she was old enough for classes, Jane went to the exclusive Brentwood Town and Country School. There were only about a hundred pupils, but many of them were the children of stars such as Gary Cooper and Laurence Olivier, so Jane did not attract any special attention because of her parents.

Each morning, she would meet Sue-Sally at the school's front gate, and they would go in together past the school nurse, who made everyone stick out his tongue for inspection and say, "Ah." After the morning Pledge of Allegiance, everyone faced east, held out his arms in greeting, and recited a "Salutation to the Dawn."

The school insisted on firm discipline, and Sue-Sally's mother often helped to provide it. She would sit Jane on her knee and give her lectures. Jane was rambunctious and was developing a temper as well, even though her mother believed that "children should be seen and not heard." She became a tomboy and, pretending to be a cowboy, raided Indian villages with Peter, making cavalry charges and riding her wooden carousel horse to noisy battle. The farm was the Fonda children's private world, and except for school or trips to the beach, they seldom left it or needed to.

In 1945, World War II ended when the United States dropped the atomic bomb on Japan. Although Jane was still a small child, it made a deep impression on her.

"I remember when the atomic bomb was dropped, and I remember the complete confusion. Dad came back from the war and did a radio show called 'The Fifth Horseman of the Apocalypse.' It was a reenactment of [dropping atom bombs on the Japanese cities of] Hiroshima and Nagasaki. And it was just a total shock to me that we could have done this.

"We had won the war in Europe, we had won the war in Asia, but we had done it because we dropped the first atomic bomb. The war was over, but now there was a new terror for me, which was this atomic bomb and how people melted and were irradiated and there were deaths long after. The radio play was a very graphic reenactment, and it really impressed me."

Another thing that impressed her later was the way public opinion was manipulated or changed at different times. For example, during the war the Soviet Union had been our ally against the Nazis, but when the war ended, some troops were stationed in Europe permanently to guard against our new enemy, the Soviet Union. "We had fought against a common enemy, but now the Soviets were described as a Communist threat. It seemed like a complete reversal."

Another way public opinion was influenced then was by stereotyping. Jane can remember hearing her family's Japanese maid talk about having relatives in a detention camp in the United States. She now thinks such camps would not have been possible if the Japanese had not been dehumanized during the war—turned into a kind of nonhuman enemy. In movies and cartoons they were portrayed in a way that made people frightened and suspicious of them.

"I believe that kind of propaganda is what made it palatable to drop an atomic bomb on Japan," she says. This is a significant point, because the same kind of dehumanization of the enemy was done many years later in Vietnam. It is easier to bomb people, for example, if you say they live in an area called "the Iron Triangle" than if you call them peasants who live in "the fertile farmland at the mouth of the Mekong River."

Jane was nearly eight years old when her father returned, and she found him almost a stranger. While his work as an actor kept him as busy as before, now she was old enough to be frightened when he grew a beard for a part and confused when he shaved it off again. What did Daddy *do*?

When she saw him on the screen, he often seemed to be a cowboy. It was hard to understand that he didn't go off all day to ride the range or that his cowboy movies were "just pretend" and not the same as home movies of "real life" that showed him plowing up the garden on his tractor.

"I spent my childhood wanting to be a boy, because I wanted to be like my father," Jane said years later. When she was as old as twelve, she still wore her hair cropped short and was enormously pleased when someone asked her, "Are you a boy or a girl?"

When he could, Henry sought time to relax with his favorite hobbies—gardening, painting, and carpentry—and he often needed to be alone. It wasn't always convenient to have Jane trailing after him, asking questions and trying to be "helpful." When he got tired of answering, he wouldn't tell her to go away; he simply stopped answering and ignored her. If she persisted in asking a question again, his jaw would set stubbornly, and the silence would continue.

"I loved him desperately," Jane said another time. "I was very much under his spell. . . . We wanted the intimacy he had with his pals, but it never happened."

His pals were business associates like Leland Hayward and Joshua Logan, or fellow actors. They'd get together for late-night card parties and bull sessions, and she'd parade in for attention. Then, as likely as not, she'd be spoken to sharply and sent back to bed feeling hurt and rejected.

One of Jane's earliest friends was Leland Hayward's daughter, Brooke. The girls had become constant companions after their fathers left for war, and their two families seemed like one. One day Brooke came over to play and said that her parents were getting a divorce. Brooke's attitude was "grin and bear it" casual, but Jane was thunderstruck.

"It seemed like the worst thing that could possibly happen," she recalled years later. "It just seemed terrible. The feeling I got was like the ground opening up and falling down a big, dark hole. I was traumatized. If it can happen to her, I thought, it can happen to me. And where does that leave me? It just seemed like a tremendous thing. And Brooke was like a sister to me. It was really close to home."

Already, there were noticeable problems with the Fonda marriage. Frances and Henry were very different people, and the difference in their interests had only been increased by the years they were separated during the war. She had a sophisticated society background and liked to be part of a crowd. He came from farm country, was moody, valued his privacy, and liked to be left alone. They patched things up as long as they could, but children can tell when something is wrong. Jane's response was to get chubbier.

And then everything changed. Henry, tired of making movies he didn't care about just because his contract said he had to, decided to return to the theater. That was where he had started and where he had received his training as an actor. He also wanted to return to doing a complete show every night and hear the applause of a live audience.

In February 1948, Henry went to New York to star as the title character in a new play about the kind of military experiences he had recently been through. Called *Mister Roberts*, it was a comedy about a quiet navy lieutenant who was stuck on a small cargo ship in a remote area of the Pacific when he wanted to be transferred to combat duty.

The play was a hit. In fact, it ran on Broadway for three years, so the only way to keep the family together while Henry was in the show was for everyone to move from California.

Jane, who was only ten years old, loved the flight to New York and loved the city streets filled with people and traffic. The Fondas' new house in Greenwich, Connecticut, was less than an hour away from Henry's theater on Broadway and near Jane's maternal grandparents as well as an aunt and uncle. Since the Fondas had moved after school was out for the summer, Jane and Peter had plenty of time to explore their new surroundings.

Around the long white house were twenty-three acres, including "lakes and swamps and apple orchards and a haunted house," Jane remembered. She loved the new kinds of trees and plants and how green everything looked. "So it didn't take long for me to forget California." At least at first, she found everything new and exciting. Peter felt differently.

"When we left Tigertail [Road], it felt like we'd been booted out of Paradise," he said later. He showed his unhappiness by writing "I HATE THE EAST" in large letters on every wall of the house. His father made him go around and erase it all.

While there were many things Jane liked, there were also drawbacks. For one thing, she was expected to abandon her wild tomboy ways and start wearing dresses, even if she didn't want to behave like a "young lady." And there was more.

"It was a rotten summer," she said. "I broke my arm. I got blood poisoning. I had an ear infection from diving in the country club pool, and to top it all off, I realized that my parents' marriage was falling apart." The one good thing that happened was that Brooke Hayward moved in nearby, along with her mother and sisters.

Until she was in third grade, Jane had been called "Lady Jane" by her family and friends. Even the name tags in her clothes said "Lady Jane" or "Lady." Then one day she stood up in front of her class and said that her name was no longer "Lady," that it was "Jane," and nobody could call her "Lady" anymore. Then she took all the name tags off her clothes. "There was a big deal about my standing up in front of class," Jane recalled, "because I was sort of shy."

Yet when Brooke greeted her in Connecticut for the first time, she called out, "Lady Jane!"

Using the childhood name might have been simple affection, but the reply it brought was icy cold: "My name is Jane— J-A-N-E, if you don't mind." And while Jane was glad to see her friend, even that couldn't make the general situation any better. Because, on top of everything else, relations with her father were becoming difficult.

"He was always making us feel guilty," Jane said about the way he treated her and Peter. "He'd scream and ask, 'When are you going to straighten out?'" At other times there would be long silent periods, which could be even worse. One night, Henry, Peter, and Jane went to the circus and sat through the entire performance without saying a word.

"He didn't buy them hotdogs, cotton candy, or treat them to souvenirs," said someone who saw them suffering. "When the circus was over, they stood up and walked out. I felt sorry for all three of them."

At the same time, Frances had became distant, and Jane drew away from her, convinced that her mother didn't love her and that she'd had always loved Peter better because she had always wanted a boy. But Frances had other problems. Her poor health made her increasingly unhappy, so she checked into a rest home and stayed eight weeks, coming out just before Christmas and then returning. Meanwhile, Jane and Peter stayed with their grandparents. Frances's mother, Sophie, was a lively sixty-three and loved Jane completely. That was some consolation.

In the fall, Jane and Brooke started school together at the Greenwich Academy. Although Jane was in the sixth grade, she had never been a celebrity before. Now her teachers and the other students treated her as someone special because of her famous father. It was a heady experience, and Jane responded by leading the other kids into mischief and becoming the class cutup.

In the spring, Frances had kidney surgery that left her with a foot-long scar that she hated. But at last she felt her health problems were resolved and could look forward to regaining her strength. Jane's half sister, Pan, graduated from high school in June and married later that month. The couple planned a honeymoon in Europe and asked Frances to go along, thinking the change of scene would help her recover. But Frances developed a lingering cold in Paris which sapped her strength and delayed her recovery.

While Frances was gone, Jane and Brooke organized a pet show to raise money for the Red Cross. They had fifty entries and lined up several distinguished judges, including Henry, who was still playing in *Mister Roberts*. Jane did a lot of growing up that summer, becoming taller and losing weight, but she also managed to get Brooke and herself kicked out of the Girl Scouts for improper conduct: Jane flushed all the merit badges down the toilet. Scouting seemed goody-goody, and she couldn't relate to it when there were so many things happening at home.

"It was boring," Jane said. "My mother was in a mental institution. I was living with my grandmother and an aunt, and an uncle who was extremely alcoholic. My father was having an affair—with this twenty-one-year-old woman. I mean, it was a pretty terrible time, so I was acting out."

The woman in question was Susan Blanchard, a beautiful blonde Henry had met at a party. After thirteen years of marriage, he had decided he wanted a divorce. Shortly after Frances returned, Henry told her the news. Jane found out on the way out the door to school one morning when Frances wiggled a finger at her, said, "Come here," and added, "if anyone tells you your mother and father are getting a divorce, say that you already know."

"And that was it," Jane said. "She sent me to school. Never said another word about it."

Already shocked by Henry's announcement, Frances was further upset when Pan, five months pregnant, lost her baby just before Christmas. After a grim holiday season, Frances had a nervous breakdown in early February. On April 15, 1950, suffering from severe depression, she took her own life.

"Very sorry," said the note Frances left for her mother, "but this is the best way out."

2

"I WAS TERRIFIED OF ACTING"

"I came home from school and put down my books," Jane said, describing what happened the day her mother died. "My grandmother stood at the top of the stairs. I really couldn't see her face.

" 'I don't want you to go out,' my grandmother said. 'Your mother is sick.' But then, my mother was always sick. They were forever telling me that. I had a date with my girlfriend Diane to go riding, so I left, anyway."

The funeral had been held that afternoon, with only Frances's mother and Henry present. Frances's mother suggested to Henry that the children be told their mother had died of a heart attack, and he agreed.

When Jane returned from riding, her father told her the news. She stood up and said, "I want to go to my room." Once there, she sat on the edge of her bed and wondered why she couldn't cry. "How weird," Jane remembers thinking. "I'm never going to see her again, and I can't cry." She went back downstairs.

That night, Fonda's face was white with emotion, but he insisted on going ahead with his performance in *Mister Roberts*. "It's the only way I can get through the evening," he said. Then he gave a performance that looked, to people who had been there every night working on the show, identical to the one he always gave.

The true story was kept from Jane and Peter. It wasn't until the next fall that Jane found out what had actually happened. It was Brooke who told her.

"I was in a history class," Jane recalled, "and someone passed me a movie magazine that said she [my mother] cut her throat. And the next class was art class, and I sat next to Brooke. I said, 'Is this true?' And she said yes." At home, Jane was asked to keep the story from Peter, and she agreed.

In her last weeks, Frances had changed her will so that Henry would inherit none of her considerable fortune. Instead, it was divided among Pan, Jane, and Peter, with the young Fondas receiving substantial trusts, though they couldn't collect any of the money until they were older.

Her parents' marital problems and her mother's suicide had increased Jane's sense of insecurity. She did not understand what her mother had done and must have partly blamed herself, thinking, "If only I had been better. . . ." At the same time, she became even more dependent on her father's approval for fear he would try to "divorce" her, too.

Now in the eighth grade, Jane still didn't feel that she was blossoming into a beautiful woman. She thought she was fat and felt tall and gawky, calling her looks "awful." There was still a touch of the tomboy about her short haircut, which, with her pug nose, made her almost cute. But Jane didn't think so. She had a close circle of friends but often kept to herself.

One day, visiting her father in the hospital where he was recovering from an operation for a knee injury, Jane ran into his girlfriend, Susan Blanchard. Henry introduced them, telling his daughter, "I hope you'll love her as much as I do."

Jane fell for her at once. Susan's blonde hair was pulled back in a knot, and she had light blue eyes and a charming smile. Not only was she "a ravishing beauty," to use Jane's words; she also dressed well and went out of her way to be friendly. "Susan was everything I wanted to be," Jane said.

The truth is, Jane was at an awkward age, on the verge of turning into a woman but almost without a clue about how to do so. "I needed a mother," she said. "I needed a woman who could tell me about how to be a woman. You know, what was appropriate behavior, how to express myself. Someone to give me some confidence. She was my role model. I had never really had a female role model that I could learn from, and young though she was, she did provide that for me."

At the end of December 1950, just a week after Jane's thirteenth birthday, Susan and Henry were married. He was forty-five, she was twenty-two, and two months later Peter would be ten.

The newlyweds honeymooned in the Caribbean, but a few evenings after they arrived, there was a knock at the door. A message had come by shortwave radio from the U.S. Coast Guard, saying that Peter had been in a shooting accident. In those days, the U.S. Virgin Islands, where the couple was staying, were very remote. It took several boats and local planes before they could even get to a telephone to find out what had happened.

"I'm not sure if I was really trying to kill myself or not," Peter recalled later, "but I do recall that after I shot myself, I didn't want to die. And I came very close to dying."

He had been visiting friends in Westchester County, New York, and had been playing with guns. It was exactly the sort of incident they always warn you about: one of the guns went off accidentally when Peter loaded it, and the bullet went through his belly and lodged near the spine.

Peter stumbled around yelling that he'd been shot until the chauffeur scooped him into the car. Fortunately, there was a hospital in nearby Ossining, home of Sing Sing, the state prison. As Peter entered, the prison doctor happened to walk in also. He had experience with bullet wounds and knew what to do.

Even so, Peter's heart stopped beating once, and the doctor wasn't sure the boy would pull through. When Jane heard that, she began praying for the first time in her life: "Dear God, if you let him live, I'll never be mean to him again." Telling Peter about it years later, she added, "You know? I was mean to you again right away."

"I couldn't help it," she explained. "He was a rotten kid in those days. He was back to being a brat before we knew he was well. I loved him, anyhow."

Peter had three blood transfusions and was in intensive care for four weeks. When he returned to school, one of his teachers brought in a birthday cake. On it were the words "Happy Birthday to Lead Belly."

At first, Peter opposed his father's marriage, but that summer he and Jane lived with Henry and Susan near Los Angeles, where Henry was touring with *Mister Roberts*. Susan kept house, cooked the meals, and looked after the kids. It was like being a family again, and Peter soon adored Susan as much as his sister did.

Although she was still young enough to do silly, girlish things with Jane, Susan was also a sophisticated grown-up who seemed "incredibly charming, funny, and outgoing," according to Jane. Susan helped Jane learn to dress and prepared Jane to begin attending Emma Willard School for Girls, in Troy, New York—the nation's oldest boarding school for girls.

"Susan was my summer," said Jane. Together, they bought new clothes, and Jane got makeup and hairstyling tips as well.

Meanwhile, Henry finished up in Los Angeles and headed for New York again to be in another play. Jane and Peter each had a room in the five-story town house he bought on East Seventy-fourth Street, and Henry converted part of the attic into a studio where he could paint.

With Susan as a guide, Jane was introduced to hairdressers, department stores, and boutiques. New York is a magical city of wonder and delight for children as much as it is for adults, and there were luncheons, theaters, and adventures. It was a happy time.

Jane was becoming more confident when she went off to Emma Willard that fall and was beginning to feel more attractive. She also felt less shy and was soon one of the most popular girls in school. When Parents Day came around and Susan showed up, "I was so proud of her," Jane said, "I almost flipped."

"Looking back on it," she says now, "going to an all-girls high school, boarding school, was an incredible experience. It removed the need to worry about how you looked and about competing for boys or anything like that. For most of the year, except for vacation, you were in the company of extremely bright women your own age.

"The greatest lesson you take away from a school like Emma Willard is that women can do anything. And you get that just subliminally, partly because of the existence of founder Emma Willard herself and partly just because it's in the atmosphere."

But Jane was still under a lot of pressure. Not only was she trying to deal with her mother's suicide and with building a relationship with her stepmother; she was growing up and going through the normal craziness and sexual tension of adolescence. To make matters worse, she was bored. Troy, after all, is a long train ride from the bright lights and excitement of New York City.

"I remember bingeing on coffee ice cream by the gallon and pound cake by the pound," Jane says. "We bought bagfuls of brownies and gobbled them down. We stuffed ourselves with peanut-butter-and-bacon sandwiches." To combat the pounds they gained, Jane and her friends at Emma Willard sought out miracle cures from magazine ads. One of them was a chewing gum that was supposed to make you lose weight. Jane tells the story in her workout book:

"My roommate believed (I don't know if she was right) that it was because the gum contained tapeworm eggs that would hatch inside of us. We presumed that the food we ate would be devoured by the tapeworm before it was absorbed by us. Sharing life with a tapeworm seemed a small price to pay for thinness. We dutifully sent in our coupons and chewed the gum, but it didn't work. Maybe the eggs were dead. What a rip-off, we thought."

Even if the gum did not contain tapeworm eggs, "that's what we *thought* we were getting," Jane says. "I think it dramatizes how completely gross we were."

When Jane was seventeen, she discovered another weight-control technique: vomiting. She forced herself to throw up after eating. What she did not learn until years later is that vomiting causes a sudden drop in blood sugar, which leads to a craving for more food.

Jane continued stuffing herself and vomiting, often five to ten times in a single day, until she was thirty-five, though not always on a daily basis. Officially named *bulimarexia*, this eating disorder is generally known as bulimia.

"It's an addiction, like drugs or alcohol," she explains, "something I never talked about. Never." She says the only reason she finally broke her silence was that "the disease has reached epidemic proportions."

At this time Jane was also trying to persuade her father to let her move to New York City to attend school. He wouldn't even consider it. Wasn't she already attending a school that was supposed to be providing the best possible preparation for Vassar, the first-rate women's college where she planned to continue her education? Besides, she enjoyed her classes in art history and liked practicing ballet, which made her feel graceful.

At the age of fifteen, she even got the title role in the annual

Thanksgiving play, though she had mixed feelings about being the star of Christopher Fry's *The Boy with Cart.*

"I was terrified of acting," she said later. "I was shy. I was fat. I was awkward." At least those were her feelings about herself. Yet that spring she managed to find an opportunity to do some photo modeling to earn the money to buy her father a birthday present. Then she cried all night in her bedroom when he said, "Thanks," but forgot to open it.

Despite her fear of acting, Jane's original appearance at Emma Willard was successful enough that she was offered another part in her senior year, when the school put on a classic eighteenth-century comedy, Richard Brinsley Sheridan's *The Rivals.* That play involved lots of costumes and makeup, which made things easier for her as Lydia Languish, and Jane was pleased with the response she got from her performance. When she tried to tell her father about her feelings, however, he did not give her any encouragement to continue acting.

Jane graduated in 1955, after her success in *The Rivals,* and had been accepted by Vassar when she made her professional debut in the theater that summer. It all began with an inspiration from Jane's aunt Harriet, Henry's sister. Thirty years earlier, Henry had launched his career at the Omaha Community Playhouse in Nebraska. Now Harriet was involved with the group, and she wanted him to come back and star in *The Country Girl* as a benefit to raise money for a new theater. The Clifford Odets play, about an alcoholic actor and his wife, would also star Dorothy McGuire, another highly successful performer who had gotten a start at the playhouse. There was even a role for Jane.

Henry was not pleased but eventually was won over. Jane was delighted. On the flight out, she suddenly found her father talking to her seriously for the first time, as if she really mattered to him after all.

"Something about the way Jane was listening to me—as one adult listens to another—got me talking about myself and the rough time I'd had getting started in the theater," Henry said. "I'd never talked to her just that way."

In fact, Jane's father never did have the kind of serious, heart-to-heart talks most parents have with their children. Frustrated by his moodiness and silence, she believed his personal coldness meant that he didn't love her. Perhaps the real truth is that he was embarrassed by the strength of his own feelings. Certainly other people also noticed Henry's overwhelming personal reserve and considered it unusual enough to comment on. For Jane, it produced a kind of desperation that started when she was very young.

Yet years later, during an interview, Henry seemed surprised to find out that his daughter had ever had trouble realizing that she mattered to him. "Well, gosh," he said with more emotion than the words might indicate, "she gets to me."

There were only three and a half weeks for rehearsals, so their schedule was a busy one. Henry was impressed with his daughter's talent, though he didn't tell her.

"At rehearsals I was determined not to pull professional rank on Jane," he remembered, "but now and then she'd look up at me for help, and I couldn't not make suggestions. She soaked up direction like a blotter.

"In one scene, Jane had to enter crying. That isn't easy—walking on at the height of an emotional breakdown. I didn't want to watch. I didn't think she would be able to handle it. I was sure she'd just end up looking phony-dramatic. But I was the last off the stage before her entrance and the first on afterward.

"Well, Jane came on wailing and wet eyed, as though she'd just heard that Vassar was not going to admit her that fall. I couldn't believe it. I couldn't believe she was acting. I thought all her anxieties had broken through the Fonda facade and were tumbling out. But the minute she cleared the stage her face relaxed. She looked at me and said, 'How'd I do?' She didn't understand that she'd done what many professionals couldn't do in a lifetime."

Jane, incidentally, is a lot more modest about her professional acting debut than her father's praise might lead you to expect.

"It wasn't anything, really," she says. "I had no technique or experience in those days, and in the third act, when I'm supposed to make my entrance crying, I asked one of the stage-hands to whack me around, to slap me hard. And that, plus the petrifying fear and trembling I had of acting on the same stage with my father, turned the trick."

☆ ☆ ☆

When the curtain came down on the last performance of *The Country Girl*, the Fondas flew to Rome, where Dino de Laurentiis needed Henry to make *War and Peace*. Filming lasted for four months of 1955, and before it was over the pressure of such a long shooting schedule had increased the strains that recently had been developing between Henry and Susan.

Jane gradually realized that something was wrong. Susan and Henry were just too different, too incompatible, and she knew their marriage would not last. But when Susan finally decided that Henry loved acting more than he loved her, fifteen-year-old Peter was the one she told first. He was eating breakfast all alone in an enormous marble dining room when she told him she was flying home and would not be coming back. He was devastated by this news and ran to tell Jane at once. She was asleep in her room, but he woke her up and demanded to know if it was true.

"Yes," she said. "I've known for a few days." Then they talked about the fact that once again they didn't have a mother, and "it just seemed like an appropriate time to lay it all out," Jane said. So she told him the long-hidden truth about how their real mother had died. It was a pretty horrendous time for both of them.

Feeling both angry and sorry, Peter began drinking heavily and roaming the streets. "I kind of entered a state of suspended animation," Jane said. She lost all interest in social activities. "I did nothing but eat figs, get fat, and watch Gina Lollobrigida through binoculars." The legendary screen beauty was a neighbor, and while spying on her at the height of her fame may sound like fun, Jane says tartly, "It wasn't."

When Susan left, she took the kids with her so Peter could return to school and Jane could begin her studies at Vassar that fall. They were glad they didn't have to choose sides. Henry was left alone with a houseful of servants. But although he called Susan several times and begged her to return, it was over. On the rebound, Henry began keeping company with an exotic Italian, Afdera Franchetti, whom he found "totally unpredictable and glamorous."

Since Vassar is in Poughkeepsie, New York, Jane was able to make weekend visits to Susan on East Seventy-fourth Street. At school, Jane's favorite subjects were French, music, and art history. At first, she studied hard and had few close friends, though she was popular and even admired because of all the movie stars she had known. Also, once again she and Brooke Hayward were classmates. Brooke had been at an elite school in Virginia while Jane was at Emma Willard. Since they hadn't seen each other in several years, there was a lot to catch up on.

For many of its student body, Vassar's main appeal was that it was near a number of leading men's colleges. "Everyone was in such a hurry to get married!" Jane remarked. "If you didn't have a ring on your finger by your junior year, forget it!"

By the time Jane turned eighteen that December, she had achieved nearly her full height of five feet seven inches. The dormitory food wasn't bad, but heavy on starch. Jane would have been heavy on starch, too, except that her bulimia continued and most of what she ate didn't stay down.

Another weight-control gimmick she discovered at this time was "diet pills," which can create a dangerous addiction. In those days, the true extent of the danger was not well known, and Jane never had trouble finding a doctor to prescribe what she wanted. Not knowing the risk she ran, she didn't stop taking diet pills "until I realized I was losing control of my life."

"At the time, I had no idea how much damage I was doing to myself, not just physically but to my state of mind. I didn't realize how destructive eating patterns made it more difficult for me to have normal and intimate relations with people or even live a normal life. Looking back, there were so many wasted years, so much time down the drain because of this horrible disease, that at the time I didn't even realize it was a disease. It took me a long time before I was able to kick it."

One reason for this obsessive interest in dieting was that Jane had begun to realize that young men were attracted to her. She began dating heavily, to the point that it even interfered with her studies. When Henry returned from Europe, he was not pleased. Already worried about Peter's increasingly erratic behavior, he didn't want to have to deal with Jane's problems, too.

For her part, Jane had read about Henry's affair with Afdera Franchetti in the newspapers and was furious. She felt this relationship was unfair to Susan—they were not yet divorced— and that her father was not being honest with her because he had not told her about Afdera himself.

When summer rolled around, Henry and the kids rented a house at Hyannis Port, Massachusetts, on Cape Cod. He was to be the guest star in *The Male Animal*, a popular comedy about freedom of speech, at the Dennis Playhouse—the theater where he'd been working back in 1928 when he met his first wife. Jane was playing the ingenue, and had never had a happier time with her father than during the three weeks of rehearsals they had together. And on opening night, Henry learned something new about Jane.

"When she came on," he noticed, "the audience reacted in an almost physical, audible way—a straightening up and intake of breath." And they didn't know she was his daughter, so that wasn't the reason. "She had presence. You either have it or you don't have it, and Jane had it." He was impressed. "But, of course, I never let her know that."

One night, as Henry stood backstage, he watched Jane's exit and was so lost in admiration that he forgot to go on. The last time that had happened, he said, was twenty-five years earlier, "when Margaret Sullavan came on in a seaweed brassiere." Jane noticed him standing in the wings "with that wonderful silly grin he gets," his face shining as he watched her. "It was beautiful," she said.

Jane had also played in Sheridan's *School for Scandal* earlier that summer, but when the vacation was over, she still hadn't made up her mind about acting. Henry always seemed to be discouraging her, and she couldn't decide whether that was because she lacked talent or because he was trying to protect her from the kind of struggles he had faced in his own career. Despite these uncertainties, she did appear in a student production, a verse drama from Spain that made her uncomfortable.

"By then," she explained, "I was conscious enough to look for things in the character, but I didn't know how. There was nothing behind the emotions I showed. I didn't know how to show that the emotions came from something and that the words had meaning." Interestingly, the problems she was confronting in real life were also confronting her as an actress.

"I was brought up where people didn't express what they really felt," she said. "You hid everything. You hid your fears and your sorrows, and your pains, and your joys, and your physical desires. Consequently, I was a zombie, living somebody else's image, and I didn't know who I was."

She may have learned this from Henry, who used his acting as a mask to hide behind and carried his own emotional secrecy to an extreme. "He was so guarded that for the first year I knew him," Afdera wrote later, "he didn't even shave in front of me. He would get up . . . wash, and then tidy the bathroom so carefully it looked as if no one had been there."

In March 1957, Peter and Jane attended their father's wedding to Afdera at his New York town house. It was his fourth marriage, and his bride was only twenty-four—twenty-eight years younger than Henry; Jane herself was all of nineteen. Jane and Peter joked about Afdera's youth when they were sure their father was not around to hear. They mused out loud that his future wives would continue to get younger until finally they would need to be fed from a bottle.

Afdera may have been young, but she knew her way around. In comparison, "Jane was almost a child," she said, describing her as "a nice, wholesome, puppy-fat teenager, ripening quickly." Afdera also says she felt that Jane "was touched by a magic star—and she was learning, very, very, fast."

Peter was best man at the wedding, but he didn't like it much. In his eyes, Afdera was hardly a replacement for Susan, and he complained that she couldn't even speak enough English to carry on a conversation. Once Henry and Afdera had left again for Europe, he became heavily involved with drugs. When Jane found out, she had him shipped off to Omaha to live with an aunt and uncle who could supervise him. Their first step was to have him see a psychologist who did a series of tests and discovered that Peter's IQ was over 160—high enough to be rated "genius." Even though he had never finished high school, the University of Omaha invited him to join its sophomore class.

The weekend after the wedding, Jane rebelled in her own way by hitchhiking from Vassar to Yale to visit a boyfriend, and she didn't bother to obtain permission first. Normally, a stunt like that might have gotten her suspended, but instead, school authorities decided she had run off because she was upset about her father's marriage and forgave her.

True, she was upset about her father's marriage, but that wasn't why she had left, and she didn't think it was right that she should be forgiven. "I've always been ashamed of privilege," she once said, and in her view, the school authorities were lenient only because of who she was—Henry Fonda's daughter. She became very disillusioned about getting preferential treatment and even about being a student at all.

"I had very good teachers," Jane said. "I just wasn't able to study." Feeling that she was wasting her father's money by not taking full advantage of the educational opportunities that were offered, she began a campaign for permission to drop out and go to Paris instead, to study art and learn French. Finally, Henry gave in.

That June, shortly after her sophomore year ended, Jane and several of her friends flew to Europe. They joined Peter and others at the white stucco villa that Henry and his new wife had rented for the summer. Located on the French Riviera, the house had lots of room, numerous guest houses, and a swimming pool, as well as a steep stairway leading down to the Mediterranean. Nearby was the charming and ancient town of Villefranche.

Soon the place was hopping with Afdera's jet-set friends. She'd often entertain twenty people for lunch and more at dinner. Eventually, Henry found such a life too hectic and got tired of feeling like a guest in his own house. "It was the craziest, most insane marriage anybody ever got into" was his summing up.

While life at the villa was indeed hectic, "it was sort of fun for a while," Jane decided, though she hated "the fakiness." Even Peter was "perfectly sweet," Afdera said, even though he didn't appreciate her. Peter felt he needed his father's friendship and that Afdera came between them somehow.

And how did Afdera think she treated Jane and Peter?

"I was very friendly with them, you know. I was like a sister. But I wasn't motherly. I wasn't understanding, but I brought them a whole new world."

Well, that was true enough. She introduced them to Jean Cocteau, who was a leading artist, poet, novelist, and filmmaker. They went to the studio of Pablo Picasso and watched him paint. Greta Garbo often dropped by for lunch and frequently swam in their pool. There were certainly compensations.

That fall, Peter returned to Omaha and Jane moved to Paris, settling into a furnished apartment in a dark building run by an elderly countess who provided room and board for young American girls. The building was within sight of the Eiffel Tower, in a fashionable part of town, and midway between a famous landmark, the Arc de Triomphe, and a famous nightclub, the Trocadero. Jane hated the place.

Everything was covered in plastic, she complained, and everything smelled. Worse, "young ladies were not supposed to talk at the table." Another problem was that despite the language classes she had taken, Jane did not know enough French to understand what her art instructors were saying. She soon stopped going to class.

Instead, she began hanging out at bars and cafés, meeting people and learning the language. One of the people she met was George Plimpton, who let her hang out at the famous literary magazine he edited, the *Paris Review*.

Jane did odd jobs for the staff, ran errands, and picked up all the latest sophisticated chitchat she could. She did her best to keep up with Plimpton and his friends, an international collection of poets, artists, filmmakers, and intellectuals whose fast-paced conversation fascinated her.

Plimpton's friends spent a lot of time partying all night. One evening at Maxim's, one of the best restaurants in Paris, Jane saw film director Roger Vadim for the first time. He had "discovered" Brigitte Bardot and made her a star, and also his wife. Vadim was famous for feature films that had a more frankly erotic side than most Americans were comfortable with in those days. That night, he was having dinner with his second wife, film star Annette Stroyberg, but when he noticed Jane, his glance lingered, and he did not forget her.

Just after Jane's twentieth birthday, Henry got wind of his daughter's activities. Furious that she was no longer attending classes and was living an enthusiastic social life instead, he ordered her back to Seventy-fourth Street.

"I went to Paris to be a painter," Jane recalled, "but I lived there for six months and never opened my paints. I was nineteen, an age when you know you are not happy but you don't know why, and you think a geographical change will make your life better."

"I enjoyed painting," she added later, "and I had a certain amount of talent. But basically I was using painting as an excuse to get away in order to try to discover who I was." She was looking for something to do with her life, discovering what possibilities the world might hold for her. But she carefully avoided the theater in her investigations. "I was frightened to death of it."

Angry at being ordered home, Jane quickly signed up for classes in French and Italian, piano, and painting to show that she was serious about her education. She also got a part-time job at the New York office of the *Paris Review* and tramped from one end of Manhattan to the other, stopping in every bookstore in an effort to get their managers to buy ads in the magazine. She also found work as a secretary for a Broadway producer.

As if Jane were not already busy enough, a friend asked her to do some modeling for a fashion magazine, and when she accepted, that led to other modeling offers. The attention was nice and the work was fun, but Jane still didn't think of herself as attractive. Mostly, she was trying to please her father with all the hard work.

"Underneath everything, I still thought about becoming an actress," she confessed. "That was what I wanted to do more than anything else, so I spent a lot of time figuring why I shouldn't. My impression, from growing up in Hollywood, was that actors tended to be a rather egotistical lot. So I said to myself, Hey, you're egotistical enough, you don't want to become even more so, so acting isn't for you. Besides that, I didn't think I was pretty enough, and I was still quite shy. The truth is, I was just afraid to try."

3

WORST ACTRESS
OF THE YEAR?

During the summer of 1958, the Fondas rented a house at
Malibu Beach in California, where many other movie-industry
people lived. Not far from the Fondas, for example, were Lee
and Paula Strasberg and their daughter Susan, who was about
Jane's age. The two had become friends in New York, where
Susan had been appearing in a play with Henry. Each day, Jane
and Susan would go swimming or driving together or would
hang around talking.

One day on the beach Susan asked, "Why aren't you an
actress?" And Jane finally thought, Well, why not? Although she
had been thinking about it secretly for a long time, when she
finally decided to commit herself, it did not seem exactly like a
major career decision. "It was kind of like something to do," she
said later.

What made this conversation especially important was that
Susan's father was one of the most famous acting teachers in the
world and had worked with many top stars, including Marilyn
Monroe. Monroe often visited the Strasberg house that summer
for coaching as she prepared for an important role in a new
comedy, *Some Like It Hot*.

Lee's classes in New York were at a place called the Actors
Studio. Only the most talented actors and actresses were ac-

cepted at the studio, and there was a long wait to get in. However, Lee also started teaching private classes, and Jane thought perhaps she would like to start that way.

The kind of acting Lee taught was based on a system created many years ago in Russia by Konstantin Stanislavsky and often called "the Method." The idea of the Method is to find aspects of your own experience that you can use onstage to understand a character in a deep way. If you know what that character's hopes and fears are and what he or she really wants, then you can try to feel that way yourself when you say the character's lines.

At least that was the theory. Henry Fonda, who was certainly a famous and well-respected actor, didn't think any of it was necessary. In fact, he once called the Method "useless garbage."

Jane went to talk to Paula Strasberg. Then she was interviewed by Lee to see whether she could be a good pupil. He could tell that she was looking for something to do with her life and wanted very much to be a success, even though it scared her to go into a field in which her father was the best.

"The only reason I took her was her eyes," Lee said. "There was such a panic in her eyes." He wanted to help her, and Jane was glad he chose to take her on as a student. She considered it a sign that someone really did think she had some talent.

When she told her father she was planning to study with Strasberg, he was not happy. Henry came from the old school, where you learned on your feet. Before he ever came to Hollywood and became a star, he had performed several hundred parts in summer stock. But by the time Jane came along, that kind of opportunity wasn't as common. There were far more actors competing for a smaller number of roles, so you had to be much more professional right from the beginning.

"On top of that, I felt that I didn't want anyone to say I got roles because I was Henry Fonda's daughter," says Jane. "I wanted to feel inside myself that I had technique and that I knew what I was doing. In a way, it was more for my own self-confidence that I felt I wanted to study. And it did give me self-confidence. If other people took two classes a week, I took four classes a week. If other people did one scene a month, I would do two scenes a month. I worked twice as hard because I knew it was going to happen to me faster—which it did.

"By the time it happened, at least inside me I felt I had proven myself to myself. But in the beginning Dad was very much against it. He would look at me disparagingly when he would come home and see me practicing my sense-memory exercises on the couch in the living room.

"For example, I had chosen in my first exercise to do a sense memory of drinking orange juice. I must have squeezed fifty oranges in order to practice how much the cup would weigh with orange juice in it, what the orange juice would smell like as it approached my face, and what it tasted like on my tongue so that I could do it without a glass and without the juice and still actually experience the whole thing. He thought I was nuts.

"The purpose of the exercise is to train your concentration. He believed that you just learned by doing, that you didn't have to go to class and do exercises.

"One time, I remember, he was in a play and in the top of the second act he made an entrance that was quite effective. I said to him afterwards, 'How do you prepare?' And he looked at me, you know, disparagingly, and said, 'I think about the grocery list.' Now I know that it's not that he's right or wrong or that I'm right or wrong but that everybody has their own way of doing things.

"In order to probe as deeply as I like to as an actress, I have to concentrate and get into a state of mind consciously. I wouldn't be able to think of a grocery list and just walk through the door. I'm not saying that makes me better; it's just the way I am. It's a very important realization for me to face the fact that although he was my father and I adore him, what was right for him wasn't necessarily right for me."

Henry didn't approve of Jane's need to study the Method, but he did keep his eye on her progress. There she was one morning, making faces at the orange juice. There she was, coming in from class and looking so confused she almost seemed to have a giant question mark above her head like someone in a comic strip. And then one day it all sank in. Henry thought it was almost as if a giant lightbulb had been turned on above her head.

Jane worked hard at her classes because she was afraid of looking like an idiot when she did an exercise or scene in front of the other students. Although she felt that many of the other students had more acting ability than she did, she also knew that she had something else: star quality, personality, and stage presence. She also had determination. If she was going to be severely criticized, at least it wouldn't be for holding back.

But while Jane was afraid of what the other students thought of her, they were afraid of her at the same time. It had to be a little intimidating to be in the same class with someone who carried such an aura of Hollywood glamour. But even though Jane worked hard, she did not want acting to take over her life and leave no time for anything else. To her, no profession was as important as that, so she continued to model for advertisements and magazine covers.

Despite suffering from what she called "major, *major* self-doubt," she began getting cover assignments for major fashion magazines, such as *Vogue*, and making fifty dollars an hour—top wages in the late 1950s. It surprised her that she could be so successful as a model, because she still thought of herself as "plain Jane," someone who was attractive, but more pretty than beautiful.

Not only did she continue to be worried about her weight; she now had even more reason to be haunted by the idea of slimness. While at the Actors Studio, she lived on cigarettes, coffee, diet pills, and strawberry yogurt. Today all that is left of that regimen is the yogurt and an occasional cup of coffee. On-screen, it may look as if she still smokes, but she's not using real cigarettes. "I would throw up now if I had to smoke a real cigarette," she says. Instead, she uses a substitute that she gets at a health-food store.

As a model, she even added another unhealthy gimmick to her arsenal—diuretics. These little "water pills" were supposed to shrink her body by forcing out fluids. What she didn't know then was that they also wash out important minerals and can be extremely damaging to the kidneys.

But if Jane was dissatisfied with her looks, others were not. Before long she was getting opportunities to use what she had learned. In her first year as a professional actress, Jane played in two Broadway shows and had a starring role in a Hollywood movie, *Tall Story*. Because she was a Fonda, many doors opened for her. Once those doors were opened, though, the name was not enough, she had to perform. And since she *was* a Fonda, she had a lot to live up to, and more was expected of her; it would not be enough just to be mediocre.

Once she started acting professionally, Jane found new reasons to admire her father. He always managed to be true to himself, whether he was on stage or film. When Jane experienced how hard it is to remain natural under artificial conditions, she was even more impressed with his work. And he was equally impressed with hers.

Before long, Henry was saying things like "There's no question but that she's going to be a bigger star than I am," and "Jane has made more progress in one year than I have in thirty." That was high praise, but it didn't turn her head because Jane never heard those words from her father. He made those remarks to a reporter during an interview, not to her.

Jane's first movie role was a starring one, offered by director Joshua Logan, an old friend of her father's. Logan had seen her photo on the cover of the July 1959 issue of *Vogue* magazine. *Tall Story* was a silly romantic comedy in which Jane played an intelligent student in love with a college basketball star portrayed by Anthony Perkins, just before his next performance—in *Psycho*—made him a star.

Logan thought that working with Jane was fun, but she didn't enjoy it, since she generally blamed herself for anything that went wrong with the picture. But even though the movie wasn't a success, people noticed her. "With her talent and a few years' experience," predicted one British film magazine, "she could easily become as famous as her father."

While waiting for filming to begin, Jane filled the time by playing in *The Moon Is Blue* for two weeks at a New Jersey theater. And when *Tall Story* was finished, she returned to the stage to make her Broadway debut in *There Was a Little Girl*, which opened February 29, 1960. Directed by Joshua Logan once again, she played a rape victim in what one critic called "an unsavory melodrama." Her father didn't want Jane to be in that kind of role, but she was afraid to turn it down for fear she wouldn't be offered any more parts.

Although the play was not a success, Jane's performance commanded respect. She was only twenty-one years old, but the New York *Daily News* critic compared her to a legendary stage actress, predicting that she could become "the Sarah Bernhardt of 1990." Since *Tall Story* was in movie theaters at the same time, Jane had good reason to feel proud that she was becoming a professional like her father, who was appearing in another Broadway play at the same time. In addition, both the New York Drama Critics Circle and *Theater World* magazine named her the most promising new actress of 1960.

Jane's next role was a part in a play that her agent had warned her to turn down. The play, *Invitation to a March* by Arthur Laurents, opened on October 29, 1960, and ran for nearly four months—a respectable hit. Before it was over, she even managed a brief foray into television, starring in *A String of Beads* on February 7, 1961.

In this ABC color special, based on a story by novelist Somerset Maugham, she played a woman who buys a string of cultured pearls and wears them to a party where everyone mistakenly decides she's wealthy. Jane did not enjoy the experience and didn't return to television again for more than twenty years.

She nearly didn't return to movies, either, because Hollywood still considered her an all-American "girl next door" type and she found that was the only kind of part she was being offered. "I just said, 'Forget it, I'm not coming back to Hollywood.'" What changed her mind was that in April 1961 she was offered a role that was too good to resist—the part of Kitty Twist in *Walk on the Wild Side*.

"Kitty Twist is a wonderful acting part," Jane said. "She's like a cat, ends up ratting on everybody and getting everybody killed. I never would have thought anyone would offer me this kind of part." Not only did it help her avoid being typecast in the future, she says. "It gave me the opportunity of playing several very, very different [emotional] colors.

"It took place during the Depression, and at the beginning of the movie she [Kitty] was mistaken for a boy, something I could relate to quite well. And she ended up in a whorehouse in New Orleans looking exceedingly glamorous and being a real bitch. It was a wonderful challenge to me as an actress. That's why I took it."

Jane made two other films that year as well. First came *The Chapman Report*, directed by George Cukor. He had been responsible for many of Hollywood's greatest films, most of which had famous actresses in them, and was known as a "woman's director." Even his bad pictures, and this was one of them, were always very stylish and elegant.

Enjoying her work, Jane began saying nice things about Hollywood again. For example, "I really love it now and may be here all summer. I never enjoyed working so much before." And Hollywood was saying nice things about her, too. George Cukor's opinion was that "I think the only thing she has to watch is that she has such an abundance of talent she must learn to hold it in. She is an American original."

In her interviews during that period, however, Jane offered some controversial opinions. "I think marriage is going to go out, become obsolete," she told gossip columnist Hedda Hopper, who professed to be shocked. It was just an idea she'd had, thinking out loud during a conversation, but the headline read "JANE FONDA THINKS MARRIAGE OBSOLETE."

She explained later that sometimes she told columnists things just to attract attention. In 1962, however, her father was in the midst of divorcing Afdera. He didn't like the kind of attention Jane was causing, didn't like the kinds of parts she sometimes chose—a rape victim, a prostitute—and most of all, he didn't like some of the disrespectful things she was saying about him. It wasn't so much that he objected to Jane's thinking critical things about him; he just didn't like her saying them. "After all, I am her *father*," he said. Later, Jane actually stopped giving interviews for a while because she knew they pained him.

While Jane was in California working on *The Chapman Report*, a major fire blazed in her former neighborhood, completely destroying the old Fonda home on Tigertail Road. When her grandmother Seymour, who had been living there, called to say what had happened, Jane was more emotional than her grandmother was. Jane felt that her whole childhood had gone up in smoke.

The other picture she made in 1962 was a Tennessee Williams comedy called *Period of Adjustment*, about the first twenty-four hours after a wedding. In this case, the bride and groom find everything going wrong. As the nervous southern bride, Jane was very funny and demonstrated both confidence and a good sense of comic timing. While the picture wasn't much, Jane's performance was "full of delights," according to influential critic Stanley Kauffman, and she confessed in an interview that "somehow making movies gets to you."

That August, Jane flew to Athens, Greece, and began working on *In the Cool of the Day*, which critic Kauffman called "an insurmountable disaster" and costar Peter Finch said he didn't mind that it was a soap opera, which could at least be fun to watch, but it "wasn't even *good* trash." The film was followed by another low point in Jane's career: her third Broadway play. Called *The Fun Couple*, it opened October 26, 1962, and closed after only three performances. The *New York Post* commented, "Even the sight of Miss Fonda in a bikini doesn't rescue *The Fun Couple* from being an epic bore."

Later that year, Jane was named Miss Army Recruiting of 1962. It was the kind of publicity stunt that agents like to arrange, and Jane went along peacefully and even gave a little acceptance speech in which she told officers and recruiters that the country needed a strong national defense. Soon after, a group of students at Harvard University selected her to receive their annual award as "Worst Actress of the Year" for her performance in *The Chapman Report*.

Jane made her last stage appearance in an all-star Actors Studio revival of Eugene O'Neill's *Strange Interlude*. One of the few authentic masterpieces of the American theater, it won a Pulitzer Prize in 1928 but is rarely performed because it is a difficult play and nearly four hours long. The play has nine acts; Jane, playing part of a pair of young lovers (the other was Richard Thomas, later famous as John-Boy in "The Waltons" on television) didn't come on until nearly the last one.

Jane's next picture was *Sunday in New York*, a silly sex comedy in which she again played a "girl next door" type. *Time* called the movie "eyewash." In his review, Stanley Kauffman observed that Jane had both talent and personality and asked the important question "What will become of her?"

It was a question worth asking. Jane was not an instant star; she had to work to achieve the awards and international recognition she has received. That she had delivered four quite different performances in her first four pictures was a sign that she could play a variety of different roles without resorting to acting formulas or to the use of a limited number of predictable mannerisms. But she was beginning to feel trapped in the Hollywood system and still too much in her father's shadow.

Thinking that a return to Europe might help her find herself, Jane flew to Paris to make a picture with Alain Delon, a popular French leading man. Jane always liked being in France, anyway, a country that adored her father and thought her beauty was "a revelation." They considered her to be "the perfect American," which was a welcome contrast to the way she had been received in Hollywood. When Jack Warner, of Warner Brothers, had first seen her, he said Jane would have a good future if she would dye her hair blond, reshape her face, and use padding to build up her bust.

Jane took a translator along to France and for the next two months did not speak a word of English. Unfortunately, the picture she made, *Joy House* (or *The Love Cage*), used lots of improvisation instead of a finished script. When shooting was finished, Jane commented, "There was too much playing it by ear for my taste."

More important than the picture, however, was that while she was in Paris, director Roger Vadim began to think of adding Jane to the cast of a new movie he was making. Although it had been years since he had noticed her at Maxim's in Paris, he had not forgotten her. Now he decided Jane was just what he was looking for.

Vadim had married Brigitte Bardot when she was eighteen and quickly made her an international star, partly by photographing her when she was wearing few clothes or none at all. After Bardot fell in love with the leading man in one of her pictures, she and Vadim were divorced. His next two wives were also beautiful actresses whom he made stars. (Actually it was only one wife, since he never did go through a ceremony with Catherine Deneuve, even though they had a son and lived together for several years.) All this was very interesting to the newspapers and made him quite a scandalous figure in America.

Jane had heard terrible things about the way Vadim chased women. When they first met, she thought he was putting on an act, because she didn't see any sign that the stories were true. When he talked to her about appearing in his new movie, she was surprised to discover that he actually seemed rather shy. Eventually, Jane did agree to make a picture with him, *Circle of Love,* and before it was finished they had fallen in love, even though there was an eighteen-year difference in their ages.

At first, Jane had been apprehensive about Vadim as a manipulator of women, but after she got to know him she felt that was ridiculous. "I discovered a very gentle man," she said. While many Americans are "always having to prove their strength and masculinity, Vadim was not afraid to be vulnerable." After he published an autobiography called *Memoirs of the Devil,* she scoffed that Vadim was "about as devilish as someone's old grandfather; he's like a comfortable old shoe."

"Nothing is more attractive than vulnerability in a woman," was his view, but while each was attracted to vulnerability in the other, Jane was very much afraid of being vulnerable herself. She had built walls to protect herself ("as high as the Great Wall of China," Vadim said) because she still doubted her own beauty and talent and even her own capacity for happiness.

During this period, Jane began to restore and remodel a farmhouse she'd discovered in tiny Saint-Ouen-Marchefroid, population 102, near the town of Houdan, about thirty-seven miles from Paris. The old stone house, built around 1830, sat in the middle of three acres of land and was quite run down when she bought it. Jane wanted it to be quaint and charming on the outside but thoroughly modern within, so she had the insides torn out and kept workers busy trying to understand her instructions for rebuilding it the way she wanted.

Besides guest rooms and an indoor pool, film-editing rooms were installed, and a projection room was added where Jane sometimes watched two movies a day. It was here that she watched some of her own pictures and also caught up on some of the famous movies she had missed, including many of her father's best-known films. Although Jane had always known he was one of the most famous and respected actors in America, she had never actually seen much of his work.

The movie of his that impressed her most was *The Grapes of Wrath*. Made in 1939, it was the third of three landmark pictures Henry Fonda had filmed that year with director John Ford. The first was *Young Mr. Lincoln*. The second, *Drums Along the Mohawk*, almost could have been about Henry's own ancestors in colonial America carving a life out of the wilderness.

The Grapes of Wrath was a powerful cry for simple human dignity and justice. Based on John Steinbeck's Pulitzer Prize–winning novel, it was about dirt-poor Oklahoma farmers struggling to survive in the "dust bowl" during the Great Depression of the 1930s. The movie drew rave reviews from the critics and won Ford an Oscar for best director. Jane Darwell, who played the mother, also won an Oscar for best supporting actress. As Tom Joad, curiously, Fonda did not win an Academy Award, though he invested the character with a fundamental decency that seemed to catch something important about the spirit of the nation.

Shot in stunning black-and-white images by cameraman Gregg Toland, the story ends with Tom and his mother separating, then a final, indelible image of him walking down the road at dawn to seek a better life.

Before he leaves, Tom's mother asks what will happen to him, and Joad says that if he dies, "then it don't matter. I'll be all around in the dark. I'll be everywhere, wherever you can look. Wherever there's a fight so hungry people can eat, I'll be there. Wherever there's a cop beating up a guy, I'll be there. I'll be there in the way guys yell when they're mad. I'll be there in the way kids laugh when they're hungry and they know supper's ready. An' when the people are eatin' the stuff they raise, livin' in the houses they build—I'll be there, too."

If it wasn't the conscience of the world speaking in Nunnally Johnson's script, it was at least the conscience of America. Jane was overwhelmed when she saw it. "I think it's the most brilliant acting I ever saw," she said. "It's a perfect movie. . . ."

☆ ☆ ☆

Filming on *Circle of Love* was completed the first months of 1964, shortly after Jane's twenty-sixth birthday. That spring, Jane and Vadim traveled to the Soviet Union. Vadim was half Russian, and his father had been a Soviet diplomat. Jane was surprised to find that the Russian people were not the monsters they were painted in the United States. "I was amazed how friendly and kind and helpful they were," she said.

The couple spent that summer together at St. Tropez, a fashionable Mediterranean resort not far from Villefranche, where Jane had stayed a few years before. She was relaxed with Vadim and found him refreshing. He wanted to get married, but she was afraid to make a commitment. While they were wrapped up in each other, the U. S. Congress passed the "Tonkin Gulf Resolution," giving President Lyndon B. Johnson broad war powers in Vietnam, and the civil rights movement was in full swing.

Jane's other object of attention that summer was the filming of *Cat Ballou*, which turned out to be her first real hit. In the picture, Jane's character, Katherine "Cat" Ballou, joins up with a drunken outlaw played by Lee Marvin (who won an Oscar for his performance) to get revenge on the men who killed her father. It was a standard-issue western—except that it was hilarious, with every cliché of the genre being played for laughs. Jane had been tempted to turn down the role, but Vadim thought Cat was "courageous, but tender, modern, and funny." He recommended that she take the part.

While Jane was shooting the picture in 1965, she and Vadim rented a house in Malibu. And since they were living together without being married, there was a lot of talk. That October, Vadim visited Jane on location in Colorado. One of her costars recalled, "This Frenchman in horn-rimmed glasses reading *Mad* magazine—all by himself" while Jane was filming.

When the shooting was over, Jane went back to France, where she continued to work on the farmhouse while waiting for the opening of her and Vadim's first picture together, *Circle of Love*, which was scheduled for March. Then a seventy-foot billboard was put up in Manhattan to announce the New York premiere. It consisted of a huge picture of Jane lying on a bed and wearing nothing at all.

Some people were outraged, but no one was more outraged than Jane. Not only had she not been aware of the ad, she didn't want people to think she would make the kind of movie the ad made *Circle of Love* seem to be. "Jane revealed only her shoulders," Vadim protested later, and you could see more of Jane in the ad than you could in the movie itself.

Jane sued the theater owners for the billboard ad, demanding $3 million for her suffering. That got more publicity. And when the billboard's owners threw a piece of canvas over it to cover her bare behind, newspapers had an excuse to run a photograph of the controversial ad all over again. They were having a field day. Eventually, the billboard was taken down and the case settled quietly, but the incident was not quickly forgotten.

When *Circle of Love* finally opened, audiences saw a sophisticated story about various love affairs, with a screenplay by the distinguished French playwright Jean Anouilh. They were disappointed to find that it didn't contain the kinds of scenes they expected. Also, it had been shot in French and then dubbed into English, which looked funny. People thought Jane did well enough; they just didn't like the movie, which fared better in Europe.

Despite the good notices Jane had received for *Walk on the Wild Side*, all of her major successes so far had been in comedies. *Cat Ballou* had confirmed her comic talents. It was a masterpiece of satire, and she'd been praised for doing every goofy thing required of her with a sweet sincerity that had audiences laughing out loud. But they were still waiting for Jane to prove herself as a dramatic actress, and the next picture she made didn't help any.

Critics said *The Chase* was too heavily serious and too full of political messages. A big-budget picture about bigotry in a small Texas town, it had a screenplay written by playwright Lillian Hellman and was well meaning but "a disaster of awesome proportions," in the words of *Life*'s Richard Schickel.

Jane played the unfaithful wife of Robert Redford, who was being chased by a lynch mob that Marlon Brando, as the sheriff, was trying to hold off. While Jane approved of the movie's theme, the real reason she wanted to make it was to work with Marlon Brando. Not only was he near the height of his career and possibly the biggest male star of the day, he also was another student of Lee Strasberg's.

"He will not settle for anything less than the truth," Jane said admiringly. "People say he's difficult. . . . I suppose he is sometimes, but he won't settle for something less than what he feels is right. I don't have that kind of courage, and that's why I admire him so much."

☆ ☆ ☆

When filming was over, she and Vadim returned to their house in Malibu, where they lived a few months of each year most of the time they were together. Visitors often expected all kinds of wild goings on, but instead found a happy couple living quietly. Jane prepared their dinners herself, practicing French-style cooking and enjoying the chance to be a homemaker. While she no longer believed that marriage was obsolete, she wasn't in a hurry for it, either.

"I love Vadim," she said. "He's wonderful fun to be with. He's taught me enormously, but why in heck should I marry him?" She wasn't sure either of them was made for family life and was afraid that getting married would spoil things. Instead, he went back to France while she made *Any Wednesday*, a forgettable comedy in which she played the mistress of a millionaire and was allowed to wear her own wardrobe of designer originals instead of specially designed costumes. Vadim kept in touch by telephone from Paris, holding at least one long conversation with her each day.

Knowing him was beginning to change her. When a reporter asked what was most important for a woman to remember about relationships with men, Jane went into some detail. "I think honesty is the most important thing," she replied. She said the secret is "to be able to say anything, to be able to hear everything, to talk about everything. . . . It's when you don't communicate, when you don't exchange, when you start sitting on grudges, that you start harboring anger. Then the little things build up. . . ."

When the picture was finished, Jane rejoined Vadim in Malibu, where they often entertained foreign visitors as well as members of the local movie crowd. Those who came to meet the famous French director found him friendly, charming, and an excellent host. Finally, even Henry stopped by to see for himself.

"He had never met Vadim," Jane recalled, "and he wanted to dislike him. He came into our house expecting God knows what after all the things he had heard—an orgy, I suppose. But there I was slopping around in blue jeans, and Vadim was sitting on the deck fishing, one of Father's passions in life." That certainly helped make a good impression.

Vadim later described his relations with Jane's father as "superficial but very pleasant." He was clearly surprised that Henry was such a private person. "He was a reserved, polite man," Vadim recalled, "totally averse to any allusions to his private life," someone who could be completely embarrassed by any kind of personal question, such as "whether he got up early or occasionally had nightmares."

Even though Vadim managed to win Henry over, Jane's father continued to condemn her unmarried status, and she knew that it hurt him. Finally, Jane was ready to accept Vadim's proposal. They chartered a private plane and flew to Las Vegas with Vadim's mother, Peter, Brooke Hayward, actor Dennis Hopper, and a very few others. Henry sent a congratulatory telegram from New York, where he was tied up in rehearsals for a new show. Vadim had forgotten a ring, so they had to borrow one at the last minute, and his mother was so busy taking photographs of the city that she missed the ceremony.

The wedding took place in a room at the Dunes Hotel, with music provided by an orchestra of female violinists. The date was August 14, 1965.

4

THE BEST OF TIMES,
THE WORST OF TIMES

Soon after the wedding, Jane and her new husband flew to France and settled into their farmhouse. Jane continued to make improvements—planting a small forest around it and building a henhouse, badminton courts, and the like. She also continued to make movies. The second one she made with Vadim was *The Game Is Over,* which has a swimming-pool scene in which Jane is partially nude for three and a half minutes. When it was time for rehearsal, she insisted that someone lock the door so that no unauthorized visitors could get in.

However, without her knowing it, a photographer hiding in the studio took a number of pictures of her. When Jane found out, she was furious, and even more angry when she discovered they were going to be published in an American men's magazine. She sued the magazine and was in the newspapers again, but eventually lost the case.

Meanwhile, America was changing. Although the "summer of love" was not until the following year, already hippies in brightly colored clothes were advocating that people "drop out" of mainstream society. As an alternative, they created an underground culture of love, rock music, and drugs as a rebellion against a way of life they considered conformist, oppressive, racist, and warlike. Society fought back against "permissiveness" and "anarchy" any way it could.

In August 1966, Peter Fonda was arrested for possession of marijuana. Some of the drug had been found in a house he was renting, and even though Peter said he didn't know it was there, the prosecutor was unrelenting. Both Henry and Jane stood by Peter, and she flew back and forth between California and France, encouraging him. By the time the charges were dropped, the incident had drawn the family together—at least for a while.

But long-haired hippies wearing "love beads" and startling outfits were only one sign of a profound spiritual struggle that was going on in the United States. The women's movement was beginning, and the foundations were being laid for many of today's environmental, racial, sexual, and "new age" concerns. The first nationwide student organization, Students for a Democratic Society (SDS), had been started a few years before by a man who was later to become Jane's husband. And a growing movement was protesting the United States's involvement in the Vietnam War.

Back in 1890, the French conquered Indochina, a long S-shaped country on the southeast edge of the Asian mainland. During World War II, the Japanese had invaded and occupied the country until September 2, 1945. That same day, the leader of the local resistance movement, Ho Chi Minh, joined with other nationalists in declaring the creation of the Republic of Vietnam. But the French had other ideas, and the United States and Great Britain supported the French.

Immediately, all factions within the country united in opposing the return of the French. In 1946 the French bombed the port of Haiphong, leaving 6,000 Vietnamese killed or wounded. Four years later, the French asked the United States for assistance. And during the four years after that, the United States supplied more than two and a half billion dollars' worth of equipment as well as 200 air force technicians to service the French combat planes.

Finally, the war became centered on a remote military fortress held by the French, who believed it could be successfully defended forever. There were 11,000 foreign troops stationed there, but four times that many Vietnamese opposed them. The siege continued for fifty-four days. Then, on May 8, 1954, the world was stunned when the French surrendered their "impregnable" fortress at Dien Bien Phu.

But when the peace treaty was drawn up by Western nations, the people of Indochina didn't get to say much about it. The 1954 Geneva Accords divided the former colony into Laos, Cambodia, and Vietnam and then divided Vietnam again, into the Communist North and the non-Communist South, supposedly only until things could settle down and there could be free elections.

Jane had been only seventeen then and like most kids her age was largely unaware of what was going on. But when she returned to the United States after *The Game Is Over*, Vietnam was in the middle of a civil war. U.S. forces had been actively fighting on the side of the non-Communist South Vietnamese for some time, and a growing number of U.S. citizens felt the United States was guilty of grossly improper interference. In the 1950s, President Dwight D. Eisenhower had warned that he could imagine "no greater tragedy than for the United States to become involved in an all-out war in Indochina," but that's exactly what was about to happen.

The United States worked to ensure that the promised free elections were never held, and the situation deteriorated from there. In 1963, there were 15,000 U.S. military advisers in Vietnam. (By 1969, there were 543,000 U.S. soldiers there.) Emperor Bao Dai had been replaced by Ngo Dinh Diem in a rigged election. When nationwide protests grew into civil war, Diem declared martial law.

Many historians doubt that President John F. Kennedy would have been able to keep the United States out of Vietnam, but before he made his fatal trip to Dallas in November 1963, he told a leading antiwar senator, Wayne Morse of Oregon, "You may be right," and promised a thorough review of U.S. policies in Vietnam as soon as he returned. Alas, events turned out otherwise.

In August 1964, there was a report that two U.S. destroyers had been attacked in the Gulf of Tonkin. Years later, a Senate investigation disclosed there had been no such attack and that the United States fired first, but President Johnson, apparently believing otherwise, vowed he was not going to be the first president to lose a war and demanded Congress pass a resolution giving him the right to retaliate. Thus, the war entered a new phase, with the United States more deeply committed than ever to doing what the French had failed to do—what, in fact, no outside army had succeeded in doing in four thousand years of trying.

While that was happening, the United States was also going through its "long, hot summer" of civil rights activity, a time when Rev. Martin Luther King, Jr., led boycotts and demonstrations, and thousands of activists from the North went to the South to register black voters. Often these civil rights workers were harassed by local whites who were opposed to integration and afraid of what would happen if black men and women had a fair chance to participate in the political process. Many of these heroic volunteers were threatened or shot at, and several were murdered—including three college students killed by a Mississippi sheriff and others. (This incident was the true-life basis of the 1988 film *Mississippi Burning*.)

Those events were very much on people's minds in the summer of 1966, when Jane was working on *Hurry Sundown*, a story about honest, hardworking black farmers trying to buy the land they worked on and meeting resistance from the rich white landowners. It was the first picture ever made in the South with black actors in important roles, and racial tensions were severe. First, the state of Georgia would not allow them to film there, even though the story was supposed to take place in Georgia. Then they moved the production to Louisiana, and things got downright nasty.

With this background, rumors had started even before the cast and crew showed up in the city of Baton Rouge, Louisiana. People said Hollywood was going to make a movie about "niggers gettin' the best of us white folk." When the black and white workers in the production unit all stayed at the same motel, there were threats by mail and telephone. Diahann Carroll, one of the picture's black stars, said the hostility was "so thick you could cut it with a knife."

"We had this swimming pool at the motel" Jane recalled, "and I'll never forget the first day one of the [black] actors jumped into it. . . . People just stood and stared like they expected the water to turn black." When the Ku Klux Klan demanded that the "niggers" all move to a separate motel, Jane and the rest of the cast said they would stop work in protest if any attempt was made to give in to such a demand. The situation was so tense that state troopers armed with shotguns were called in to guard the motel night and day.

Things were even worse in nearby St. Francisville, Louisiana, which had been picked as the "typical southern town" needed for the movie. It had fewer than a thousand residents. Unfortunately, it was also a center for Klan activity. The townspeople, however, generally stayed far away from the outsiders, peering at them from a distance as if the movie people were Martians who had just landed.

"You never saw anybody," said Robert Hooks, another black actor. "You could feel their eyes watching you behind lace curtains, though. Like they could cut your heart out."

One day when Vadim was visiting, he and Jane went for a walk through town, along with a photographer. A little black boy ran up to them and gave Jane a flower. Charmed, she bent down and kissed him. Immediately, the entire streetful of people stopped talking and turned to stare silently, filling the air with sudden menace.

"They don't seem to like you kissing blacks," Vadim said.

"Don't be silly," Jane replied. "He's only a child."

But an hour later the sheriff showed up and told everyone to get out of town "for their own safety." He gave them just thirty minutes after they finished the scene they were filming. As they drove off, two of the cars were hit by bullets that shattered their windshields. Later, Vadim said Jane had given the boy a $60,000 kiss, since a full day's shooting was lost. Yet after all that effort, the film was terrible. Rex Reed recalled that a fellow critic had said "that no film is ever so bad that you can't find some virtue in it. He must not have seen *Hurry Sundown*." Another reviewer called director Otto Preminger's taste "atrocious."

Jane's next movie was *Barefoot in the Park*, a frothy Neil Simon comedy about newlyweds. It costarred Robert Redford, who had played the same part in the original Broadway cast. The play had been a huge success, and the film version became Redford's most successful picture so far, launching him to superstardom. While Jane was working on this picture, her father married for the fifth and last time. He had finally found the ideal wife for himself: Shirlee Adams, an airline stewardess and model just a few years older than Jane. Before long, the two women became close friends.

☆ ☆ ☆

When Jane returned to France, she found that many of her French friends were angry about what was going on in Vietnam and often expressed anti-American sentiments. Since Vietnam had been a French colony, they considered themselves experts.

When Jane replied that there were a lot of good things about America, her French friends argued rings around her and came up with facts she had never heard before. They said Jane just could not see the truth because she was an American and that blinded her to faults all the rest of the world could see.

"I defended us," Jane said, "because I could not believe our country was doing anything wrong. I could remember the Second World War from when I was a child. And I could remember letters my father wrote me from the Pacific. I knew that was a war we all believed in. In my earliest memory of this country, we were the heroes, so I couldn't believe that what we were doing in Vietnam was wrong. There had to be some misunderstanding.

"It doesn't happen to every generation, but we were part of a generation where something was happening that turned us upside down. And the way a person reacts when everything they believe in is turned inside out is, I think, very profound. But it isn't always very diplomatic, very polite, very calm, or very rational. In my case, I reacted with rage, with absolute rage—because I had been a believer. I had believed that this country did not do bad things. And the extent to which I truly believed that was also the degree to which I felt rage when I discovered that the opposite was true.

"I think if I had not been so idealistic about the country I wouldn't have been so angry when I began to realize—see, I had been living in a country that had occupied Vietnam and fought there before we did. These were people who had been through it. Some of these people had actually lain on railroad tracks to prevent the troop trains from leaving for Indochina carrying supplies. I resented the fact that they were 'holier than thou,' criticizing our country when their country had been there before us. And I realized I didn't know what I was talking about. That was when I began to read."

On January 30, 1968, the North Vietnamese Tet offensive against U.S. forces began. On February 8, when U.S. bombs totally destroyed the Vietnamese village of Ben Tre, an American officer at the scene explained, "It became necessary to destroy the town in order to save it." On French television, Jane saw the ruins of Vietnamese hospitals and churches that had been destroyed by American bombs. Some of her French friends said, "Look what your country is doing. You're bombing civilian targets." And they ridiculed the officer for saying the village had been destroyed in order to save it.

In self-defense, Jane began to read books about current issues so that she could learn for herself what was really going on and come to her own conclusions. One of the most moving books she read was a short, simple, and terrifying account called *The Village of Ben Suc* by Jonathan Schell. In it, the distinguished reporter calmly described how the peasants of Vietnam were being destroyed by U.S. soldiers in a war where military targets were not all that soldiers attacked.

Despite her growing concern about the war, Jane found time to enjoy her several dogs and cats and her farm in France as well as the ducks, rabbits, and pony she kept there. She was also a busy hostess. Bardot, Deneuve, and Stroyberg—the other women in Vadim's life—were frequent visitors, and Jane enjoyed playing with his children. Soon she was wondering whether it wouldn't be a good idea to have one of her own.

While she thought about it, she and Vadim made another picture, a science-fiction spoof of uptight attitudes about sex and nudity. This was her crowning achievement as a brainless beauty, though the character she played is anything but stupid. The movie was *Barbarella*, based on an inventive and erotic comic strip that was widely popular in France. Jane, of course, played Barbarella. During the film, which takes place in the far future, she wears twenty beautiful and revealing costumes, though there were supposed to be twenty-one.

When filming began in Rome, Italy, in late summer of 1967, the final outfit failed to arrive. Vadim told Jane that anyone who'd read *Barbarella* would expect her to be naked all the way through, so he suggested they start out with her naked. After all, that was the kind of movie people would expect from him, anyway. "Everybody will be waiting for that," Vadim argued, "so why don't we get it over with right away and get on with the picture?"

He told Jane the shot of her naked would just be at the very beginning, while the title and opening credits were rolling, and he promised that the letters would cover her up. When she complained that they didn't do a good enough job, he dutifully went back and did them over to meet her objections.

"I don't think of it as an erotic film," Jane told interviewers at the time. "It's just funny and free and nice." And it was, because among all the special effects and scenes of life in the year A.D. 40,000, there was Jane, looking as wholesome as apple pie. During the 1970s she went through a period where she felt tremendously guilty for having made the picture, but later was able to see it as almost a pre-feminist tract and at least a picture with "a certain charm and freshness." When it came out, crowds lined up all over the United States to see *Barbarella* spread across the screen in CinemaScope. Henry's response to the film helps put it in perspective.

"Jane," he said, "has survived more bad movies than any actress should be able to in a lifetime." Today people renting it at a video store and expecting a camp classic are often disappointed to find that it is far better, far more fun and entertaining, than many pictures that promise more and deliver less. One thing audiences did not know is that Jane had become pregnant while the picture was being filmed.

During her pregnancy, Jane became more interested in political affairs. In October 1967, up to half a million people marched on Washington, D.C., to demand an end to the war in Vietnam. In November, she began to follow news of Lord Bertrand Russell's International War Crimes Tribunal in Stockholm, Sweden.

Although it was ignored or scoffed at in the United States, the tribunal was taken quite seriously in Europe. Many of the participants were very distinguished, and the tribunal amassed an overwhelming amount of evidence from a wide range of witnesses, even the children of Vietnamese peasants. From the tribunal and from other sources, Jane began to learn about the 100,000 tons of napalm that had been used in Vietnam up until that time, the 4 million pounds of bombs being dropped each day, and the 8 million people kept prisoner in massive encampments.

Meanwhile, her father went to Vietnam as part of a troupe of performers to entertain the troops. "My eyes were opened," he said on his return. Henry found the soldiers had high morale and he thought the only problem was dissent at home. "Obviously we should be there, and the job is being done and it's a good job." It was several years before he changed his mind about this assessment. Until then, he spent a lot of time on fairly bad terms with both Jane and Peter, at least partly over similar political issues.

Although she was pregnant, Jane saw no reason not to continue working. Her next movie was *Spirits of the Dead*, the last film she made for Vadim and the only one she ever made with Peter Fonda. The movie consisted of three short stories, each presented by a different director. Mostly, it's memorable for showing Jane in a lot of skimpy costumes. She was working on it when she got the news that on April 4, 1968, Martin Luther King, Jr., had been gunned down in Memphis, Tennessee.

"1968 was a turning point for the country," Jane says, "It was the year of the Tet offensive in Vietnam, when the American embassy was overwhelmed by Vietnamese soldiers. We had been told all this time that the war was winding down, and suddenly we realized there was a good chance we were not going to win.

"It was a year of major uprisings all over the world. That May in Paris, students joined with workers and almost overthrew the de Gaulle government. I mean, I was living in the middle of a situation where it suddenly looked as if the government of the country might be overturned by people my own age. Everything was in turmoil. Everything was turned upside down. And that was when Vanessa was born."

Although living abroad, Jane kept up with developments back in the United States, where Sen. Eugene McCarthy (called "Clean Gene") was seeking the Democratic party's nomination for president on an antiwar platform and openly opposed Lyndon B. Johnson, who later decided not to seek reelection. Another antiwar candidate, Robert Kennedy, brother of the slain president, was murdered in Los Angeles just minutes after winning the California primary.

That summer at the Democratic National Convention in Chicago, the violence continued. It became clear that not even within the Democratic party, at least at that time, could the wishes and aspirations of these Americans be heard. Outside the convention hall, more than ten thousand demonstrators chanted, "The whole world's watching," as police attacked with clubs and tear gas, beating everyone within reach—including newsmen with expensive cameras, innocent bystanders, and even convention delegates who got in their way. Inside, CBS newsman Dan Rather was punched by convention guards and then hustled out of the hall while continuing his live broadcast to a nationwide television audience of horrified Americans.

In the presidential election later that month, Nixon was elected by a wide margin. While the truth about the Nixon White House is still coming out, much that is now known to be fact would have been considered utterly incredible even in those passionate, tumultuous times. Who would have believed, for example, that as early as the spring of 1969, National Security Adviser (later Secretary of State) Henry Kissinger was discussing nuclear weapons as a way to win the war—even though he was publicly pretending to be a "moderate" influence on national policy?

Although the antiwar movement was shut out of the political process, protests continued after President Nixon was elected. A year later, on October 15, 1969, a major demonstration—a "Moratorium on the War"—was held in Washington, D.C. Although demonstrators did not know it, the government already had a plan for the massive bombing of cities and civilian areas in North Vietnam, in order to deliver what Kissinger called "a savage, decisive blow against the North Vietnamese." After the moratorium demonstration, that plan was abandoned.

"Those Americans who marched in Washington on October 15 to protest the war had no idea of their impact," writes Seymour M. Hersh in his book on Henry Kissinger, *The Price of Power: Kissinger in the Nixon White House.* "They were protesting the policies already adopted by the Nixon administration and not those under consideration. President Richard M. Nixon came out of the crisis convinced that the protesters had forced him to back down. The protesters thought the Moratorium had been largely in vain."

The conviction that they'd failed was reinforced that November when another demonstration brought out 3,700 police and 1,200 National Guard troops to protect the White House, plus another 9,000 soldiers on alert nearby in the event of an emergency. Surrounding the White House were buses lined up bumper to bumper to form a protective wall.

In a state of siege, President Nixon stayed inside and watched football on television, trying to act as if nothing unusual were happening. Meanwhile, half a million American citizens descended on Washington in cars, buses, and trains. Late one night, Nixon sneaked out to meet some of the demonstrators. They were shocked that the only thing he could find to talk about was college football.

Also at this time, as a warning to the Soviets, Nixon and Kissinger ordered the Strategic Air Command to put its B-52 aircraft on "combat-ready status" for the first time since the Cuban missile crisis in 1962. These bombers, armed with nuclear weapons and loaded with fuel, sat on runways at air force bases all across the United States.

Without any public announcement, the president had put the country on the most advanced possible state of military alert—Def Con 1—for twenty-nine days before the alert was canceled. The Soviets, fortunately, did not respond by going on full alert themselves.

☆ ☆ ☆

In September 1968, Jane and Vadim were in Paris, and Brigitte Bardot was predicting the child would be a girl with the same birthday as her own—September 28. When the day came, Vadim playfully put his hands on Jane's stomach and pretended to say a magic spell so she would have the baby. Vanessa was born that day.

"What a nice gesture of friendship," said Bardot's congratulatory telegram. Jane had never been so happy. "There was a grin on my face that I couldn't wipe off," she said. Vanessa gave Jane a very personal stake in the future of the world that she had not felt before. It's a feeling every parent can recognize, especially every mother. "Two things have changed me," Jane said, "becoming an actress and the birth of my daughter.

"I had never felt that I was maternal and had not particularly wanted a child prior to getting pregnant, but something happened to me while she was growing inside my stomach. For the first time I felt confident as a human being and as a woman, and I'm sure it was because I was finally a mother."

☆ ☆ ☆

Tired of playing sexy, simpleminded heroines, Jane had an entirely different role in her next picture. She flew to California with Vadim and Vanessa, and in January 1969 began preparing for *They Shoot Horses, Don't They?* The part of Gloria, the marathon dancer, was juicy and dramatic, demanding more of her than she had ever had to give to a performance. Without any obvious preaching, the movie was also a sobering indictment of the failures of capitalism and big business.

"This picture was the first time I had a chance to feel that what I was doing as an actress had an importance beyond just entertainment," Jane said. "Not only that, but I was working with a director, Sidney Pollack, who asked my opinion about the script. For the first time, I felt I was becoming a responsible, thinking person professionally as well as individually. And once you've had a taste of that, you can't go back."

They Shoot Horses, Don't They? was probably Jane's most depressing picture as well as one of her most acclaimed. It told of two people who meet during the Great Depression that followed the Wall Street crash of 1929 and decide to compete for a thousand-dollar prize for dancing. Quality wasn't the point of the contest, though; it was endurance. Whoever could stay upright longest would claim the money. Gloria was bitter, trapped by social problems she did not cause and could not cure. Finally, desperately tired and hopeless, she begs her dance partner to put her out of her misery, as if she were a broken-down horse.

To lose weight after her pregnancy, Jane jogged daily on the beach at Malibu and swam in the Pacific. She also began to follow a healthy diet. During her pregnancy, Jane had already abandoned the binge-purge cycle of bulimia that had secretly dominated her life since she was seventeen years old. Not only did these changes help her as an expectant mother; they helped compensate for the severe rigors involved in shooting *They Shoot Horses, Don't They?* She was so wrapped up in the picture that she even began sleeping at the studio so she could stay in character between scenes.

"I played a suicidal, manic-depressive woman, and it was hard for me to go home at night, happy as I was at being a mother, and not lose the character. I found I couldn't go to work in the morning as a happy woman and then step into that role."

Work on the picture lasted for months, and the scenes were shot in the same sequence they appear in the movie itself, unlike the typical shooting schedule in which scenes are shot according to location or other practical considerations. Consequently, a remarkable and unusual team spirit developed among the cast as they entered more and more fully into the tragic, disintegrating lives of their characters.

To help get them into the spirit of the time, Pollack showed old movies from the 1930s whenever extra time was available. In addition, Jane read the Horace McCoy novel (of the same name) that had inspired the film, as well as other books on the Depression.

For the two and a half punishing months that it took to film the picture, Jane gradually became more and more like the woman she portrayed—desperate, negative, and depressed. She began losing weight, and even when she was not on camera, Jane wandered around with a tired, empty expression, her whole body slumped over hopelessly. "Before long," said someone involved with the film, "everybody connected with the picture was worried about whether she was going to make it through."

One night, she and costar Red Buttons danced together for fourteen hours in the deserted ballroom set that had been constructed at the Warner Burbank studios. After a while, they were so tired they were able to find positions that would allow them to sleep while still dancing, just as participants in real dance marathons once had to do.

"You have to find out what there is in your own life and among your own feelings that can make the reaction of a separate person happen to you," she once explained. In this case, she succeeded brilliantly, though it was the hardest work she had done so far.

At the end of shooting, no one knew whether to laugh or cry, the company had worked together so intensely for so long. But the ensemble work paid off with three Oscar nominations for the stars—Susannah York for best supporting actress, Gig

Young for best supporting actor (he won), and Jane for best actress. It was her first Academy Award nomination, and though she didn't win, she did collect a handsome consolation prize when the New York Film Critics voted her best actress of 1969.

They Shoot Horses, Don't They? was generally considered too depressing ever to make much money, but it earned a lot of prestige for the people who made it and won awards at film festivals all over the world. Among the careers it changed was Jane's, since it revealed her—really for the first time—as an astonishing dramatic actress.

Her own view was that audiences might find a message of hope in the picture if they looked carefully enough. "If we could pull out of the Depression," she said, "we can pull out of the mess we're in now." She meant the war in Vietnam. And director Pollack basically seemed to agree. "Kids don't want to be entertained now," he told a reporter. "They're pretty cynical. Hopefully, they will find it interesting and enlightening to discover that there's been another bad time in America, even worse than it is now."

On July 21, 1969, the same day that Neil Armstrong became the first human being to walk on the surface of the moon, Vanessa stood up and took her first four steps. In August, starlet Sharon Tate and other friends of the Fondas were murdered by members of the Manson "family." Charles Manson was an ex-convict who had spent most of his life in jail and who had gathered around him a band of followers who would do anything at all for him. The murders shattered the colorful hippie vision of universal love and peace by showing that it also had a dark side.

Back when Jane had been making *Barbarella*, the life of pleasure she lived was very far removed from her father's solid Midwest values and had little to do with the political and social upheavals she read about every day in the newspapers. As she became more aware and more involved, she began to ask, "Who am I? What side am I on? Is there any purpose to my life?"

Instinctively, she was on the side of the underdogs, because that was the way her father had brought her up. But Jane needed more answers. At the time, many entertainers, like the Beatles, were traveling to India to acquaint themselves with that country's philosophers and religious teachers. Jane felt perhaps that would be a good direction for her, too.

"I needed to go away and put myself in a totally new environment in order to understand myself and what was going on inside me," she said. In October, she left Vanessa and Vadim together at the farm and flew to India. But from the moment she set foot there, she was "virtually traumatized by the poverty and suffering.

"I was—I was aghast. And every time I saw a European or American I would want to talk about it. 'Look at these children in the street, who are starving!' I'll never forget—this little kid, carrying a dead baby, begging. And the response was always the same—'Oh, come on Jane, don't be so bourgeois, bringing your American values here. You know these people are coming from a completely different place. They have their religion, their spirituality. What is poverty to you is not poverty to them.'

"And they'd continue with their chatting and all that. I wanted to join the Peace Corps and dig wells. And I suddenly realized—I'm not a hippie. I am not a hippie. I'm a practical person. I see something and want to do something about it. So that was one thing I learned in India."

Unlike many middle-class Americans in India, Jane did not discover the inner calm and wisdom she had been led to expect. Instead, she came away confused and angry. It infuriated her that Americans could see India's poverty and excuse it as part of the Hindu religion. And she was haunted by the memory of seeing that child begging with the corpse of his little brother in his arms.

In a way, although Jane did not find what she expected, that trip to India was a revelation to her. When she returned to the United States and looked out the window of her room in the Beverly Hills Hotel, all Jane could see and smell were the crowds of Bombay.

"I'd grown up here, but I never looked at it in these terms before. India was urine, noise, color, misery, disease, masses of people teeming. Beverly Hills was as silent and empty and antiseptic as a church. And I kept wondering, where is everybody?"

5

JANE OF ARC

When she returned to the United States, it was still bitterly divided on a number of important issues. On November 21, 1969, for example, a group of Native Americans landed on Alcatraz Island in San Francisco Bay. They declared the island Indian territory and occupied the deserted former federal prison there. Supported by food and other supplies donated from San Francisco, Berkeley, and other local communities, the invaders held on and gained national attention.

When Jane read a magazine article about the incident, she sought out writer Peter Collier and asked him to take her to Alcatraz so she could find out firsthand what was going on. Through Collier she also met attorney Mark Lane. Soon she was finding out the problems of other minorities as well. One of the most controversial groups she met with was the Black Panthers.

Portrayed by police as armed and dangerous revolutionaries, the Panthers were known in their own Oakland, California, communities for sponsoring school lunch programs. Their violent antiwhite rhetoric and militant defiance of authority led to clashes in which many of their leaders were either killed or arrested and imprisoned. Had they been targeted for extinction? Many people thought so.

Jane also began to become aware of the needs of GIs, many of whom had been drafted into the army against their will and did not want to go to Vietnam. They often did not know why we were there, or did know and disapproved. To help them, one-time screenwriter Fred Gardner had organized the first "underground GI coffeehouse" in Columbia, South Carolina, in January 1968. It offered food and drink, plus entertainment and support for soldiers struggling with military authority, but did not encourage troublemakers.

Soldiers could go there to discuss social issues and relax without being in a bar or having to spend a lot of money. The first coffeehouse was so successful that others soon opened near many other military bases, though they often met with resistance and harassment from local authorities.

Jane met Gardner one evening at a party and was eager to find out about his work, but he was tired and had little patience with her questions. "If you're really interested, you should go out and visit these places," he told her rudely, "the military bases, the Indian reservations, the black ghettos."

To his surprise, she answered, "Okay, I will."

She made her first stop in March 1970, at Fort Lawton, Washington, a military base some Native Americans were planning to enter and nonviolently claim as their territory. Gardner invited her to hand out leaflets, but initially she declined, saying, "I'm not ready to do that." However, Jane did talk to the soldiers and ask them, "Would you like to come and talk with me at the coffeehouse this evening?"

Twenty minutes later Jane was arrested and then was kept waiting several hours before being allowed to meet with anyone in charge. When she demanded the right to call a lawyer, she was told, "You are a civilian, and this is a military base. You have no rights here." That was too much. Jane lay down on the floor and refused to move, warning, "If you don't let me call a lawyer, you're going to be in such trouble—!" She got to use the phone.

"I hear from the GIs I've been talking to that we need a GI Bill of Rights," Jane told the press later, "and from the Indians that we need an Indian Bill of Rights. I always thought that the Bill of Rights applied to all people, but I've discovered differently."

The November 1969 newspapers had been full of the My Lai massacre—an incident similar to the one that later inspired the movie *Platoon*. Many Americans were shocked to learn that in 1968 an entire village full of people had been deliberately slaughtered, but after talking with so many soldiers who had been to Vietnam and who had horror stories to tell on the basis of their own experience, Jane was not surprised. When she tried again to tell her father about the war, however, he exploded.

"You don't know what you're talking about!" he insisted. "We don't do that. We're Americans." That was what everyone had always thought. Jane responded by bringing some Vietnam veterans to talk with him. As Jane introduced him to a series of enlisted men, officers, and even a member of the army's elite Special Forces (the "Green Berets"), Henry began to learn more about the war and gradually began to change his opinions. Eventually, he even made four one-minute television commercials calling for an end to the war.

Although it took longer for him to agree with Jane's assessment of the war, he was already impressed by her achievements. When she'd been living in France with Vadim before marrying him, Henry had hardly been able to stand it. Once he even referred to her as "my alleged daughter," as if he could hardly believe they were related. But those days were past.

"We're very close now," he boasted, "closer than we've ever been. She doesn't talk about me the way she used to any more." After years of zinging each other in interviews, they had finally begun to come to terms with one another. Jane's social life impressed him, too. "Look at the kind of home she's created," he said. "Look at the life they lead out there in Malibu—people coming, people going, all day long, open house all the time.

And Jane handling it all so beautifully, making people feel comfortable."

Included in this family closeness was Peter Fonda, who had a major success of his own in 1969—a movie called *Easy Rider* that he made with his friend Dennis Hopper and an unknown actor named Jack Nicholson. *Easy Rider* was an independent feature that explored various life-styles of the sixties. It cost only $375,000 and ended up raking in over $60 million. Terry Southern, who wrote the screenplay for *Barbarella* and other movies, worked on the script, but the real responsibility for the movie belonged to Peter: He starred in it, produced it, and had the vision and determination that created it.

At that point, the Fonda family was the most impressive acting dynasty Hollywood had seen in half a century. But events were moving rapidly around them, and before long they would all be caught up in the tides of change sweeping over the land.

In June 1970, FBI director J. Edgar Hoover proposed a secret plan to blacken Jane's reputation by having her publicly accused of threatening the president's life. He personally sent a message to his Los Angeles office telling agents there to frame her by sending a film-industry gossip columnist a phony letter that claimed Jane had attended a Los Angeles fund-raiser for the Black Panthers and helped lead a chant of "We will kill Richard Nixon! . . ." while raising money to buy weapons. The letter was never printed, and the columnist—*Daily Variety*'s Army Archerd—denied ever receiving it.

Jane visited black militant Angela Davis in jail, marched down the Las Vegas strip with welfare mothers, and picketed stores with striking grape pickers. Wearing jeans and a T-shirt, she drove from place to place in a station wagon, often finding it hard just to keep clean while living out of a backpack and sleeping on floors in different people's homes.

The Bible says a prophet is not without honor save in his own country, and Jane was certainly no exception to the rule.

But when she set out to find the "other" America that was generally hidden from view and to discover for herself the reality of oppression and discrimination, Jane began an extraordinary process of discovery. Living her life in public, educating herself in public, she naturally made her mistakes in public, too. By spreading her energies into so many different issues, Jane knew she was blamed for being superficial and not really concerned.

"I'm not a do-gooder," she informed one rally, defiantly raising a clenched fist. "I'm a revolutionary—a revolutionary woman!" But while she was sincerely trying to help people, she often did get more attention than the cause she was supporting. She was sometimes victimized, sometimes exploited, sometimes just plain wrong. She was not trying to shore up a sagging career, though, or get rich off the publicity. And she wasn't stuck on herself. "She was down-to-earth and completely open," one activist recalled, "just one of the guys. . . . Pretty soon I forgot the movie-star business and concentrated on her as a person. And as a person, she was terrific."

Gradually, Jane became grim and humorless, seeing nothing to laugh about in the massive injustice she was discovering. A newspaper report of one of her speeches complained that "she talks like a long-playing record." She knew, too, that many times GIs would visit a coffeehouse to talk with her only because she was a famous actress. That was okay with her, for they usually ended up telling her their problems anyway.

She kept on talking to people, following Fred Gardner's advice to learn firsthand about the poverty, suffering, and injustice that many people find it easy to ignore or do not even know exist in this country. And she read widely. Jane said that in those days she had "complexes about my lack of political sophistication" and admitted that "plenty of people laughed at me." But when she found out she was wrong about something, she just said, "Well, I made a mistake," and went on.

Jane kept in touch with all aspects of the peace movement

in her travels, meeting with doctors, lawyers, veterans, students, and clergy, helping to raise money and spread the word wherever she was needed.

In Fort Bragg, North Carolina, she was arrested for passing out leaflets on the legal rights of GIs. At Fort Hood, Texas, she was again arrested for attempting to distribute leaflets. She was escorted off the base and told never to return. At the University of South Carolina, she experienced tear gas for the first time as police broke up a student demonstration.

Her fourth arrest occurred at Fort Meade, Maryland. This time the military really got out of hand. Even after Jane's lawyer, Mark Lane, identified himself, army personnel deliberately smashed his tape recorder so he would have no record of what was said and done. And they did enough pushing, shoving, and bullying to give Jane a nice set of bruises to display to eager press photographers when she was finally released.

Around 1970, Jane rented "a very nice house with a swimming pool and everything" on Mulholland Drive, which stretches along the top of the Hollywood hills. Then she drove across the United States to New York to work on a film called *Klute*. Stopping at military bases, she talked to soldiers about their experiences during the Vietnam war. What she heard moved her to tears more than once.

"They really told me things that far exceeded even what I had been reading in books. These were guys who had committed war crimes and who were suffering for that and crying and trying to make some sense of it and trying to understand why this had happened to them." Jane also visited reservations and talked to Native Americans about the way they were treated by the government, the way treaties had been broken, and how their lands had been taken from them. As she drove to New York, she thought of all these things.

"At one point—as I was crossing the Rockies, I remember— it hit me that I really had a choice. I could be a sort of upper-class charity lady and not change very much about my life. You know—be a good person and raise money and live up in this big house on the hill and sort of come down from this ivory tower and dole out money and good deeds. Or I was really going to have to change. Everything. I was going to have to give up a whole way of life that I was accustomed to and completely change myself. And I decided the latter.

"In that respect, I was like all those other kids in the country, even though I was thirty-two years old. But it was the giving up of an entire way of life and a life-style. And that's the role that I chose to do for ten years. I sold everything I had. If I bought furniture, it was from the Salvation Army. Everything fit into a suitcase. I just changed my whole life and proved to myself that I could do it. I remember making that decision about who I wanted to be and what I wanted to be. . . ."

Jane sold almost everything she owned, auctioned it all off—even her beloved French farmhouse—and spent the next few years living out of a small bag. Not everyone understood this decision or approved of it, of course. Sometimes the people Jane was trying to help accused her of doing more harm than good, and people who opposed her efforts said she was a fool who had been "duped" by the "Commies." Advice came from all sides, and it wasn't easy for her to figure out the best thing to do in such extraordinary circumstances, or even what was right.

When she finally got to New York to make *Klute*, Jane began to research her part. In the title role, Donald Sutherland played a detective who falls in love with prostitute Bree Daniels (Jane) during a murder investigation. Jane spent days and nights meeting with call girls and madams and out on the streets with hookers and pimps, but when nobody tried to pick her up, Jane decided she just wasn't very convincing as a prostitute.

She went back to director Alan Pakula, saying, "I don't think I'm believable. You've got to get somebody else." He didn't share her worries on that score, though at first he had been concerned that she might be too involved politically to concentrate on playing a part and keeping up with the demands of making a full-length picture. She did spend a lot of time on the phone keeping in touch with other activists, but all Pakula had to say was "We're ready for you, Jane." Then she'd stand quietly for three minutes, focusing until she was fully in character again.

"She's totally and completely in the film, and nothing else exists," Pakula explained. "And when the scene is right . . . she goes right back to the phone, and that other world is total. It's a gift good actors have. She has it to an extraordinary degree."

What enabled Jane to play Bree Daniels the way she did was her contact with the woman's movement that had been emerging as yet another key element of the new national consciousness-raising. Far from interfering with her performance, the growing awareness and self-awareness brought about by her activism made it better.

"In the process of crossing the country, I was introduced to the women's movement, really for the first time. And as I met feminists and began to understand the women's movement, I began to identify with it. In the course of that trip I began to have questions about whether I should even do *Klute*, whether I should make a movie about a prostitute, a woman who was victimized.

"I talked to a number of women, and I wrote to a number of women and asked their opinion. Basically, what they said to me was 'If you can play this character with depth and understanding, there is no reason not to do it.' And I think it was my new consciousness as a woman that helped me bring depth to the character. It wasn't that *Klute* made me aware of the women's movement; it was the women's movement that made me better able to play the character.

"I asked questions that I would never have asked before, about why is it that women do this and what does it represent.

"One of the best scenes in the movie is where the guy is about to kill me and he plays this tape and I hear him killing my friend and I cry. I would not have cried before. I would have played fear, but I would not have had the compassion that led me to cry. That was the result of a new consciousness that I had, and it gave a new depth to the film."

Her contact with the women's movement gave Jane a new understanding of her own life, too. "Suddenly I could view my life in a totally social context," she said. "I was able to understand, for the first time, my mother. I was able to understand my [half] sister, myself, my friends, the women I know. I was able to seek out women, not just because there weren't any men around to talk to but because I really preferred to talk to women."

The result of making the picture was more than useful insights. In March 1972, the role of Bree Daniels gained her another Academy Award nomination for best actress. When it came time for the Oscar ceremonies, she was tempted at first to refuse the award if she won. Then she considered making a long, radical speech, as some of her friends urged.

Henry convinced Jane that she would make more of an impact by keeping quiet and not using the occasion as a political forum. "I implore you not to" is what he said. When she won, people worried as she walked down the aisle. Sure, her outfit was beautiful, but what would she *say*? They sat in troubled silence as she walked to the stage.

"There's a lot I could say tonight," Jane told them, "but this isn't the time or the place. So I'll just say, 'Thank you.' " The relief and the applause were overwhelming.

☆ ☆ ☆

In November 1970, after filming *Klute*, Jane gave a talk in Canada and flew back to the United States, entering by way of Cleveland, Ohio. As she came through customs, she was pulled out of line and made to wait while her luggage was searched. If she had been less tired, Jane might have wondered about receiving such special treatment, but at first she didn't notice anything wrong.

While she waited, agents seized her address book and

photographed every page of it—perhaps to see if she was smuggling any contraband phone numbers. Then they discovered some prescription diet pills and 102 plastic vials of vitamins. On top, the vials were labeled in red nail polish—B, L, and D, which stood for breakfast, lunch, and dinner. Jane was carrying the pills so that she'd be sure of getting proper nutrition even if she didn't have time to eat properly. The authorities were supposed to ask whether she had prescriptions for the pills, but they didn't. They simply busted her on the spot.

Three hours later, the agents were still waiting for a policewoman to arrive to conduct a strip search, but Jane insisted on going to the bathroom. When they objected, a scuffle ensued, and she tried to punch a special agent, but missed. She spent the night in the Cleveland jail and once again made newspaper headlines, though this time it was no fault of her own. As her father put it, "because she was Jane Fonda, the finger was on her."

But Henry did not have to agree with Jane in order to stand by her—especially when it was so obvious that she was in danger and that the government was out to get her. "I'm not unhappy she's an activist, that she is as sincerely concerned as she is," he told the press. "I'm unhappy about some of the people she is listening to." And in an interview published two months before Jane's arrest, Henry had said he did not always agree with his daughter, but, "I love her. I respect her right to say what she says."

Unlike most drug-possession cases, the one against Jane actually went to trial, where it was discovered that the special agent was not officially on duty but was moonlighting as a security guard for the airport. Also, since he was on federal property at the time but was not a federal officer, he was out of his jurisdiction anyway. Before the charges were dismissed, Jane's lawyer discovered something else significant. He managed to get one of the government witnesses to admit under oath that the local U.S. attorney's office was prosecuting the case on orders from Washington.

The reason for this was that Richard M. Nixon, president of the United States, maintained an "enemies list" of people he wanted to punish, people he had a grudge against and wanted to "get" if he could. No one outside the government knew about this list until later, but Jane Fonda's name was on it. From that moment on, the FBI had been dogging her footsteps and spending thousands of dollars to collect information about her opinions and activities. They also clipped hundreds of newspaper stories to go into her file, which was stamped CONFIDENTIAL.

At every rally where Jane spoke, secret tape recorders preserved her words, and even small gatherings were infiltrated so that detailed notes could be made. Eventually, her FBI file was more than five hundred pages thick, including records of her long-distance telephone calls, which were monitored by the National Security Agency and transcribed so that copies could be sent to President Nixon, Secretary of State Henry Kissinger, and other top government officials.

Later, she discovered that her huge FBI file had been secretly turned over to reporter Jack Anderson and that her bank records had been illegally given to the government without her knowledge or permission. Some people would say her privacy was being invaded. After thinking about the situation and consolidating her evidence, Jane filed suit against the government in October 1973. The case dragged on for almost six years before it was settled out of court.

Meanwhile, Jane discovered that the CIA had routinely been opening all mail she received from overseas and that the government had even gone so far as to put a listening device in her bedroom. She felt she was living in a police state, but eventually Jane dropped her demand for monetary damages, and the FBI issued a statement of apology, admitting what the agency had done and saying it was no longer FBI policy to do such things to American citizens.

Vadim normally kept silent about political issues because he was a visitor in this country, but after Jane's drug arrest he also spoke out in her defense, commenting, "There's a difference between politics and police harassment." He respected Jane's causes even when he thought she was going too far, but by the end of 1970 he and Jane had basically separated. Vadim had taught her a lot, even how to relax, and had given her a child, but they had drifted apart. He said he would prefer being married to "someone soft and vulnerable," and sometimes he called her "Jane of Arc," referring to Joan of Arc, the teenage Maid of Orleans who had saved France by leading an army against its enemies in the fifteenth century.

"The fear that threatened Vadim the most was that we would no longer be friends," Jane said a while later, "and that I would take Vanessa away from him. But now he knows I would never do that." In fact, he took care of Vanessa while Jane devoted herself to political activities during the next few years. Although he complained that it felt "like baby-sitting for Lenin," he continued to admire Jane's enthusiasm and dedication, calling her "an extraordinary woman."

"Jane was not seeking a new love affair," he said. "She wasn't leaving me for another man, but for herself."

6

THE WINTER
PATRIOT

Jane was involved in two important projects during this period. One was the Winter Soldier investigation, held in Detroit in February 1971. The investigation was named from a phrase in *Common Sense*, a tract written during the American Revolution by colonist Tom Paine. Paine made a distinction between "the sunshine soldier and the winter patriot"—those who stood by the revolution only when it was easy and those who were also willing to support it when the going got tough.

Like Bertrand Russell's International War Crimes Tribunal, the Winter Soldier investigation was designed to reveal what was really happening in Vietnam. There were four days of testimony, during which a hundred veterans of the war—officers and enlisted men—described what they had seen and done in Vietnam. A documentary film based on their testimony was considered too horrifying to play in any theater, much less on television.

"The thought was that for the first time, we wanted to have a war crimes tribunal on American soil, with American soldiers who had participated in these crimes testifying," Jane explains. "I spent about six months on a tour that began at the Cleveland airport, traveling around the country, speaking on campuses, and recruiting Vietnam veterans to come to Detroit to testify. I ended almost every speech with a description of what the Winter Soldier was going to be and asking any vets who were interested to meet me in a room afterwards. That's how a lot of the witnesses were recruited."

All this was happening right after Lt. William Calley had been tried for the My Lai massacre and clearly showed that what happened at My Lai was not an isolated incident. While that had been fully publicized, it was clear to Jane and others that it was only one incident among many, not some weird aberration but part of the basic policy of the United States and the way it was conducting this war.

Without trying to let Calley off the hook for what he had done, the investigation's organizers wanted to make it clear "that you couldn't blame it on the soldiers and leave out the fact that their superiors, the high-ranking officers, knew this kind of thing went on and tacitly allowed it to happen. That was the purpose of the Winter Soldier investigation," Jane said.

Among the witnesses was Ron Kovic, a Vietnam veteran who tells his story eloquently in a small autobiography called *Born on the Fourth of July*, because that is the day he was born. Perhaps he is best known today because he was played by Tom Cruise in the 1989 movie based on this book.

Kovic signed on for a second tour of duty in Vietnam, only to be wounded and return permanently paralyzed from the waist down. He was in a wheelchair when he attended the October 1968 Vietnam Moratorium in Washington. The police who arrested him weren't impressed by the Purple Heart he wore for being wounded in action. They kept telling him to sit up straight, even when he yelled in anguish, "I don't have any stomach muscles. Don't you understand?" After he took part in the Winter Soldier investigation, he told Jane, "I've lost my body, but I've gained my mind."

Jane's other major project in those days was to organize a group of entertainers to visit military bases and entertain the troops. In addition to Jane herself, Donald Sutherland, Elliott Gould, Howard Hesseman, Peter Boyle, and comedian Dick Gregory were among the early participants, but eventually most of the stars were replaced by performers who were not as well known. After rehearsals in February and March of 1971, the show traveled around the country all summer.

Since they weren't welcome on military bases, Jane and her friends performed in GI coffeehouses and high school auditoriums across the country. That fall, the show moved on to Hawaii, Okinawa, Japan, and the Philippines. It won a special off-Broadway Obie citation after it played at New York's Lincoln Center, and in 1972 it was even filmed.

Perhaps audiences wanted *Barbarella*, but what they got was a sort of political vaudeville with a number of amusing skits. Folksinger Holly Near sang "Nothing could be finer than to be in Indochina making moneeeeeey," and Donald Sutherland provided a dynamite conclusion by reading the end of *Johnny Got His Gun* by Dalton Trumbo—probably the strongest anti-war novel ever written. The show marked an important step for Jane because it allowed her to combine her performing skills with political activity.

"It was difficult for my old friends in Hollywood and elsewhere to know how to relate to me," Jane says. "I didn't look the way I used to. My interests were different. My values were different. I was very, very controversial. I had burned my bridges. And yet people in the movement had a hard time knowing quite how to deal with me because I was a movie star, and it was a very lonely time where I was in between two worlds.

"My relations with men were difficult because I was famous and I was mobile and I was independent. And it was very threatening to men, especially at that time, when things like fame and money were very much looked down upon. So it was hard for me to find men who were not intimidated by me." As a result, even though she was basically a romantic, she'd begun to doubt she would ever get married again.

"Your heart speeding up when you hear his voice over the telephone, your fit of dizziness when you see him, your feeling of loneliness when he's away. I still believe in that kind of love," she said, "because it's the most beautiful in the world." At the same time, however, she said, "I was very cynical about relationships, and I never would have thought I'd be married again and have another child."

But within a year she was keeping company with one of the most respected and influential members of the "New Left"— Tom Hayden—a man later called "the single greatest figure of the 1960s student movement" in *The New York Times.* He had done as much as any one person to create new, radical politics in America.

Two years younger than Jane, Tom had been born and raised in Royal Oak, Michigan, a working-class section of Detroit. His parents were divorced when Tom was ten, and he was raised by his mother, a school film librarian. After attending Catholic schools, he went to the University of Michigan at Ann Arbor, where he became involved in the student movement. He visited the University of California's Berkeley campus the year before some six hundred students were arrested there during the Free Speech Movement, which sparked student rebellions that have shaken governments as far away as Paris and Beijing. He also covered the civil rights movement for his school newspaper, the *Michigan Daily,* and later became its editor.

One of Tom's most significant achievements was being a founder of Students for a Democratic Society (SDS) in 1961 and the major author (he wrote the first draft) of their key position paper, "The Port Huron Statement," a year later. It was named after the Michigan town where it was written, and according to Tom, the manifesto essentially said that "society should be organized to ensure that people have a true voice and can really determine the decisions that are made." These ideas, sometimes condensed to the term *participatory democracy,* were a powerful driving force in the years ahead and continue to lie at the heart of Hayden's political activities today.

While in college in the early sixties, Tom spent one summer vacation in the South reporting on voter registration and especially on work being done by the Student Non-Violent Coordinating Committee (SNCC—pronounced "snick"). After graduation, he went to work for SNCC in Georgia and Mississippi. From there, he went on to four years of community organizing in Newark, New Jersey, working long hours for twenty dollars a week. During the 1967 race riots in that city, Governor Richard Hughes sought his advice about what to do—and followed it.

Tom was also among the organizers of the antiwar demonstrations that rocked Chicago during the 1968 Democratic National Convention. He gained new notoriety as a result, since he was one of the "Chicago Seven" indicted for allegedly crossing state lines to incite a riot.

In February 1972, after a long, chaotic trial during which the judge, seventy-four-year-old Julius Hoffman, was viewed by many to be one of the prosecutors, Tom and the others were convicted and sentenced, Tom to five years in prison. When the Seven appealed, they were released on bail, and in November their convictions were reversed. The trial was a circus, with one outrageous incident after another. Tom details the entire travesty in *Trial*, one of the seven books he has written.

Tom arranged to meet Jane in 1971, when her travels brought her to Ann Arbor for an antiwar rally. She was working on the Winter Soldier investigation at the time, and he wanted to see whether she was sincere. Jane was immediately drawn by his impish humor and calls Tom "a very funny man," though his own description is that he is "funny looking."

"Who are you living with?" he asked over coffee.

"God forbid, nobody," Jane replied.

A year later, they met again in Los Angeles. By then she

had put together a slide show on the war, focusing primarily on what the United States was doing there, the bombs we were dropping, the number of civilians who were being killed, and so on.

"The purpose of doing it was that Nixon was running for reelection as a peace candidate who was going to end the war," Jane says. "We knew that while he was bringing the troops home, he was also escalating the air war and dropping more bombs and new kinds of bombs—antipersonnel bombs that were illegal according to international rules of warfare. Tom saw my slide show and came backstage to meet me. He said at some point, 'I've done a slide show, too, and I'd like to show it to you sometime.'

"It sounds like a joke, but it's actually true. So about a month later, he came over to my house to show me his slide show. It wasn't a date. We didn't have dates in those days. And I think that's when I started to fall in love with him. His slide show started four thousand years ago in Vietnam. It began by showing you what their civilization was, one of the oldest civilizations in the world. He talked about Vietnamese legends and told how four thousand years ago they had fought against the Chinese, who had tried to invade them, and how they had won by harnessing their incredibly primitive means against the much larger Chinese army.

"All the way down to the present, he showed their history, always concentrating on their culture. And then these beautiful Buddhist women, very modest, were being changed as the United States deliberately imported pornography into South Vietnam—books and magazines and films—to set up a middle class with American values who would resist the older, traditional values. And of course with that came plastic surgery and implants to look sexier and more American.

"*The Pentagon Papers* [a book containing once-secret U.S. government reports about the Vietnam War] documents this. There was a deliberate campaign conducted by the United

States. In some ways, Tom's slide show was an even more horrifying lesson in what we were doing. It was much more devastating than mine. That fact that he was even sensitive to these cultural issues showed me what kind of person he was. But it also taught me so much more and made me hurt so much worse.

"Like the soldiers who went there, I had never taken the time to understand Vietnamese history, Vietnamese culture. I was just against the fact of war but was never really sensitized to who it was we were waging this war against."

Seeing these pictures, Jane began to cry. When that happened, Tom says, "I looked at her in a new way. Maybe I could love someone like this."

As Jane watched Tom's presentation with growing interest and respect, she also learned that there had been more than one attempt to kill him. Later, she said, "we were holding hands in the dark when Vanessa woke up and stumbled into the living room. Instead of ignoring her or saying I should put her back to bed, Tom turned on the lights, introduced himself, and took her in his arms. . . . I thought: At last, a human being."

Jane felt that a huge burden had been lifted from her because Tom, who was famous in his own right, was not threatened or intimidated by her. "He was a celebrity in the movement, trying to grapple with what it meant to be a male leader at a time when men were supposed to allow women to be equals," Jane said. "Tom and I came together as equals in that way, and that is one of the things that made it easier for us."

What Tom noticed about Jane was that "she had an intensity about her whole life."

Seeing Tom's slide show was one factor that made Jane interested in going to North Vietnam. Tom had been there twice and had the right connections to arrange such a trip. In fact, on his second trip he had brought back three prisoners of war, the first POWs to be released by the North Vietnamese, and was invited to Washington to confer with top government officials about what he had learned.

Jane wanted to know more about the history and culture of the Vietnamese people, but that was not the only reason for the trip. "I had resisted going for many years," Jane explained, "because I knew it was going to be misunderstood. But in the spring of 1972 the antiwar movement began to get reports from French and Scandinavian scientists who had witnessed the systematic bombing of the dikes of North Vietnam.

"Now, you have to understand that North Vietnam is below sea level," Jane says. "It is protected from the sea the way Holland is—by a very intricate system of earthen dikes. These dikes were built by hand by the peasants of North Vietnam. And if the dikes are destroyed, North Vietnam would be flooded.

"During the Johnson administration, the Pentagon had, among the various options that it presented to the president, proposed bombing the dikes and flooding North Vietnam. The Pentagon said this could lead to the death of a million people through drowning and starvation because their crops would be destroyed. And Johnson, to his credit, said no—no we will not go for this option. This is what Hitler did to Holland during the Second World War. We must never be guilty of this.

"Now it became clear that unbeknownst to the American people, unannounced, at a time when Nixon was holding up the peace sign and saying that he was winding down the war because he was bringing the ground troops home, he was actually escalating the war by trying to destroy the dikes. We knew what that meant. And that was why I went. That was the one reason.

"Hundreds of people had gone. Ramsey Clark, the attorney general of the United States, had just come back. But I felt that as a movie star, as someone who had access to the media, if I went I would be able to document what Nixon was doing. And that's what I wanted to do."

In February 1971, Jane passed the word to representatives of North Vietnam that she wanted to examine their situation first-hand, and they invited her to visit. But first she had some movies to make. *Steelyard Blues*, a sort of radical comedy that she made

Jane, resisting efforts to coax a smile,
seems intent on studying the camera.

On April 8, 1941, Henry, Pan, Jane, and
Frances Fonda visit family in Omaha, home of
the Omaha Community Playhouse, where Henry and
Jane would perform together years later.

*The entire Fonda family—Frances, Pan, Peter,
Henry, and tomboy Jane—gathered for this group
photo after moving to Connecticut.*

THE OMAHA COMMUNITY PLAYHOUSE

presents

DOROTHY *and* HENRY
McGUIRE   FONDA

in

"The Country Girl"

by

CLIFFORD ODETS

with

JAMES HARKER   JAMES MILLHOLLIN

JANE FONDA

Produced and Directed by

KENDRICK A. WILSON

Settings Designed by PATTON CAMPBELL

Executed by ROYAL W. ECKERT and the Playhouse Stage Crew

(THE COUNTRY GIRL is produced by special arrangement with Dramatists Play Service, Inc.)

JUNE 24, 25, 26, 27, 28
1955

MUSIC HALL
Omaha Municipal Auditorium

*Jane, far right, rehearses with her father and
the rest of the cast of* The Country Girl *in 1955.
This benefit for the Omaha Community Playhouse
was Jane's first appearance on any stage.*

*Jane starred with Anthony Perkins in
her first film,* Tall Story, *in 1959.*

VOGUE 60c

JANUARY 1

1960

NEW IDEAS
on what's important

NEW WAYS
to wear the new
colour scheme

NEW BEGINNINGS
in American
Fashion Naturals

NEW SERIES
on enduring beauty

NEW VISIONS
of the house
around you

**NEW YEAR—
NEW DECADE**

*Jane was a top New York model
while she studied acting at the
beginning of her career.*

*Jane and her husband, Roger Vadim, were
living in France when their daughter,
Vanessa, was born in September 1968.*

During their 1974 trip to North Vietnam, Jane and Tom toured the ruins of Bach Mai Hospital (left), which was destroyed in 1962, and were welcomed by crowds wherever they went.

They Shoot Horses,
Don't They? *(right)*
*was as physically
draining as a real
dance marathon.
Jane starred with Jon
Voight in* Coming
Home *(below),
a 1978 drama
about a disabled
Vietnam veteran.*

Jane, Troy, Tom, and Vanessa (in whiteface) pose with their dog, Manila, for their 1980 Christmas card.

*Jane was determined not to use
a stand-in for the diving scene in*
On Golden Pond, *the 1981 hit
in which she starred with her
father and Katharine Hepburn.*

Jane has developed many exercise programs since she first became the "queen of fitness." She now has tapes for every fitness level, including low-impact aerobics, working with weights, and fitness routines for pregnant women.

*Jane and Tom relax at their
ranch in this 1984 photo.*

Jane Fonda has seen and accomplished
a great deal in her life—one can
only wonder what this American original
will undertake next.

with Donald Sutherland, would be the last film she made in the United States for the next five years, and *Tout Va Bien* (*Everything's Okay*), another French film, was notable mainly for being the first of the many times Jane would be cast as a reporter.

When she was finished shooting, Jane returned to the United States to accept her Oscar for *Klute,* and then, in July 1972, she secretly flew to Hanoi. She visited some prisoners of war and inspected the ruins left by U.S. bombing missions, shocked by what she saw. That led to one of the most controversial actions of her life.

"I didn't go to Vietnam with any intention of talking on the radio," she said later, "but after about two days I had seen more destruction to hospitals, villages, schools, and cities than I cared to think about. I asked the Vietnamese, my hosts and hostesses, if I could make tape recordings for the radio. I said I would like to do it every morning to describe what I was seeing. . . . I said that we'd been lied to and that I didn't think it was possible to continue . . . without it destroying us as human beings. I said we really had to think about what we were doing, that we couldn't allow ourselves to be turned into robots."

Basically, she was providing a firsthand report on conditions that were well known in Europe but almost entirely unreported in the United States. But many Americans were outraged by her dozen or so broadcasts, and when they saw a ten-second news clip of her frolicking and laughing as she inspected an anti-aircraft gun, they considered that to be the last straw. Even today that is the one thing she most regrets, because she wasn't thinking about the gun as she smiled and waved; she was thinking about the group of teenage soldiers she was with.

"When you're famous, you learn in the public arena," Jane said later. "Your mistakes are played out in public, and it's painful. But I do learn from my mistakes." She has even gone on national television to apologize for some of her antiwar activities. Of course, those who had already made up their minds still refused to listen.

"I made a lot of mistakes while I was there," Jane explained. "They were made out of naïveté. They were made thinking that people would understand. I knew very well from the Winter Soldier investigation that the soldiers were kept very isolated and alienated from what was going on on the ground. They didn't even know the names of the cities. They were very alienated. And I thought if I, as an American woman, can describe what I'm seeing, maybe it will humanize the war.

"I never, as I was accused of doing, asked them to desert. I knew too much about military law. I knew I must never ask the soldiers to do something that would get them into trouble. I simply described what I saw in the hopes that they would think about what they were doing. If I had ever done anything seditious or treasonous, if I had ever done anything I was accused of doing, I would have gone to jail. I never did break the law."

Her message to servicemen who could hear the broadcasts was similar to what millions of Americans were trying desperately, emotionally, to communicate to their fellow citizens.

"I implore you," she said. "I beg you to consider what you are doing. All of you in the cockpits of your planes, on the aircraft carriers, those who are loading the bombs, those who are repairing the planes, those who are working on the Seventh Fleet, please think what you are doing. Are these people your enemy? What will you say to your children years from now when they ask why you fought this war?"

Her return was met by a storm of outrage. Picketers called her "Hanoi Jane" and "traitor," among many worse things. She received death threats, and her father got letters urging him to send her "back to Moscow." But over and over she was accused of having called for American soldiers to desert, and that simply never happened.

"I regret that I spoke out on the radio because it was misunderstood," Jane says now. "I regret a lot of what I did. But I brought back film of the dikes. And I brought back the bombs that were taken from the dikes, fragmentation bombs that caused the dikes to explode from the inside. When I arrived at the airport in Paris, and in New York, I had press conferences, and I showed the film. A month later, the bombing of the dikes stopped. Now, I can't prove that I was responsible for that. But if I had any responsibility for that, then I think that all the hostility was worth it, because I think that millions of lives were saved."

When people claimed she had been "duped" by the Vietnamese and asked if she thought she was being used for propaganda purposes, Jane replied with a few questions of her own:

"Do you think the Vietnamese blow up their own hospitals? Are they bombing their own dikes? Are they mutilating their own women and children in order to impress me? Anyone who speaks out against this war is carrying on propaganda— propaganda for peace, propaganda against death, propaganda for life!"

In California, someone tried to get the state legislature to criticize her because "she spread the lies of our enemies." Jane replied to such charges by asking, "What is a traitor? I cried every day I was in Vietnam. I cried for America. The bombs were falling on Vietnam, but it was an American tragedy."

She was delighted when a congressional investigation was proposed.

"If Congress wants my views on the war and details of my trip, I am eager to share what I have learned," she said. "Everything I do, I do publicly. What I said over the radio in North Vietnam is what I have been saying in the United States—let us stop the genocide that is being committed in our names."

It turned out that Congress did not want to hear Jane's views on the war, but that didn't stop her from spreading the word. In August, she traveled to Miami to join protesters at the Republican National Convention, where Richard Nixon was being nominated for a second term as president. This was the election where his personal campaign committee had burglars break into the Democrats' office in the Watergate apartment building in Washington, D.C., the election where wiretaps, robberies, break-ins, forged documents, and other "dirty tricks" were used to discredit anyone who opposed the president and his illegal war machine. Nixon personally supervised massive payments as part of a cover-up, but eventually failed.

At the convention, 500 members of the Young Americans for Freedom, a right-wing student group, signed a petition saying that Jane should be prosecuted because her broadcasts were "an outrage to the patriotic and loyal citizens of this country." It was all part of the sideshow to deflect attention from the real issues she was raising. And for all the rage that was expressed, she had broken no law and such opposition did not change her mind about what she had seen.

After the convention, she and Tom organized the Indochina Peace Campaign (IPC) to lobby the American people to end the war. She vowed to work "right up until election day to counter the lies of the Nixon administration and tell the truth about what the United States is doing in Vietnam." Working eighteen hours a day, they covered ninety cities in nine weeks.

"It was a grueling trip," recalled singer Holly Near, who traveled with them, "but we found a lot more people eager to hear what we had to say than we thought. Jane and Tom would speak. I would sing a song or two. Then we'd show slides that Jane took in Vietnam and answer questions. It was all pretty low key."

While this was going on, Jane was semiblacklisted in Hollywood, but she didn't entirely give up her career. Despite being busy with political issues and despite the industry thinking she was "box-office poison," she and Tom flew to Norway after the election to make A Doll's House.

Jane had the lead in the picture, which was based on an 1879 play by Norwegian dramatist Henrik Ibsen. While abroad, she revealed that she and Tom would be married "as soon as I am able to," but in order not to divert attention from their antiwar activities, neither she nor Tom would talk about the engagement publicly.

Filming took four and a half weeks during November and December 1972, but by coincidence, the story's timely feminist theme had appealed to another company at the same time, so two productions were being shot at the same time. The other one, starring Claire Bloom, failed at the box office, but Jane's efforts did not even get that far. Instead of theatrical distribution in this country, her version premiered on ABC-TV on December 23, 1973. It was only the second television work of her career, and it was not really made for television. With only minor exceptions, Jane would not act again on TV until she made *The Dollmaker* in 1983.

When their work was completed, Jane and Tom joined a large demonstration at the U.S. embassy in Stockholm, Sweden, where a counterdemonstrator splashed Jane in the face with red paint. Afterward, they flew to France to meet with the North Vietnamese negotiator at the Paris peace talks. Then, just after her thirty-fifth birthday, Jane flew to the Dominican Republic for two days to obtain a divorce from Roger Vadim.

The wedding took place January 21, 1973, at Jane's house in the Hollywood Hills. Henry and Shirlee Fonda were there. Peter, who had been married and divorced, brought his second wife. The ceremony was conducted by Richard York, an Episcopal priest, and was traditional except for one small change. Instead of Jane promising to "love, honor, and obey," both she and Tom vowed to "love, honor, and maintain a sense of humor."

The gathering was small and informal but as festive as if it were a glamorous "media event." Vietnamese students danced and sang native folk songs, and there were Irish jigs. Three months pregnant, Jane announced that she and Tom would start a truly revolutionary family—one based on home, love, and togetherness.

Six days after the wedding, a cease-fire agreement was signed in Paris and the longest U.S. war came to an end. Two million Americans had served in the war, almost 60,000 had died in it, and 1,400 are still missing in action. Of the 270,000 wounded, 21,000 returned home as disabled veterans. The nation sighed with relief, but there were no parades, and the veterans received little thanks. In the years that followed, they were neglected and forgotten by the country they had served.

"There are three reasons why the war ended," Jane explains. "One is because of the nature of the indigenous Vietnamese revolution. They have always won against every country that has invaded them for four thousand years because they were prepared to sacrifice for their own independence.

"The second reason that we lost the war is that international opinion was against us. It's important to recognize that. The world was against us.

"And the third reason we didn't have our way in Vietnam is because of the antiwar movement. In the beginning, because of the various presidential administrations, we were forced to protest from outside—march and protest and shout and scream and yell and find ways of expression that were always from the outside. Johnson stepped down rather than end the war. The Democratic party wouldn't allow the antiwar candidate to have a chance. And the Nixon administration and a whole wave, a new freshman Congress—the 'Watergate babies'—came in. Suddenly the 'hawks' became 'doves.' Cracks and crevices and fissures were created in the very foundations of the Establishment because of the dialectic of the antiwar movement and Watergate. And that is where we stepped in."

The war had been a difficult period for everyone, especially since the issues that divided the nation produced a "generation gap" that also divided families. The Fondas were no exception to this pattern, but Henry and his children had been reconciled long before the war ended.

"Peter and Jane were successful very young," he explained. "Their rebellion against me as a parent didn't last too long." He said Jane had turned into a militant overnight and "it was too fast for anyone to handle." Naturally, she had made mistakes, but,

"To tell you the truth, in many areas she's been vindicated. That war was obscene."

By April 1973, most of the troops had returned and the IPC was premiering another slide show. But when some six hundred prisoners of war came home with more fanfare than had greeted the returning troops, Jane spoke up again. A few of the POWs told stories of systematic torture at the hands of their captors, and Jane tried to set the record straight.

"It would be foolish for anyone to say there was no torture," she said, "but it is a lie to say that it was the policy of the North Vietnamese." She pointed out that the majority of POWs denied having seen any mistreatment and were being ignored. "We the people have been lied to and manipulated constantly about the war in Indochina," she said, explaining the hostility that greeted her remarks. She insisted that the POWs were no more heroic than "tens of thousands of GIs [who] have returned legless and jobless to silent airports—no brass bands, no rose-strewn hero's welcome, no White House extravaganzas for them."

Once again, Jane found herself bringing a message that wasn't a surprise to the rest of the world but which Americans did not want to hear. Yet despite all the publicity and even a series of cynical exploitation movies based on the idea of tortured POWs, Jane still maintains that it isn't true.

"I talked to a number of POWs who said that while they had suffered in prison and had been put into solitary confinement on occasion, they had never experienced—nor heard of— any systematic torture. And they particularly scoffed at the idea [spread by false press reports] that POWs had been tortured to meet with me. They told me that when it was announced I was coming and wanted to meet with POWs, the problem was to choose which ones were going to meet with me because everyone wanted to. But those POWs were not the ones who were given access to the media when they came back."

Across the country, emotions ran high. At the University of

Southern California, where some of Richard Nixon's political "dirty tricks" experts and Watergate cover-up criminals had been educated, students hanged her in effigy. A Connecticut congressman nominated her for an award "for the rottenest, most miserable performance by any one individual American in the history of our country" and called her "a spoiled brat" who "doesn't know what she is talking about."

In Tacoma, Washington, the junior chamber of commerce launched a nationwide boycott of her films, and in Dallas, public reaction forced a television station to cancel a showing of *Tall Story.* A South Carolina bill officially asking theater owners not to show her films received 643 cosponsors and was passed without opposition or debate. The Indiana state senate passed a bill urging her to "retract and apologize."

Colorado rejected an attempt to have Jane declared unwelcome in that state. A representative who introduced a similar bill to ban her from Michigan admitted, "Quite frankly, I know this bill is unconstitutional. It's just my way of telling her to go bag it." Things were even worse in Maryland, where legislators debated whether it would be better to cut Jane's tongue out or simply have her killed.

Yet Jane refused to back down.

"Why did Nixon make heroes of the POWs and not the fifty thousand men who died there?" she wanted to know. "Could it be that paraplegics don't make good spokesmen for Nixon? Voices from the grave can't congratulate the president on peace with honor."

It seemed to Jane that the POW situation was being manipulated for shabby political reasons that had nothing to do with compassion for the POWs' ordeal and even insulted the commitment and suffering of the Vietnam veterans who had not been held prisoner. Also, as far as she was concerned, this propaganda effort was drawing attention away from the real issue.

"I'm very weary of the thinking that says there are two sides to every question. There aren't. Hitler, for example, was wrong. . . . The real question is, who is ultimately responsible for the war? For those who don't already know the answer, I suggest they read *The Pentagon Papers*, which reveal that the United States has always been the aggressor in Vietnam. The idea that we were defending the South from a Communist invasion from North Vietnam was and continues to be a lie, designed to justify our invasion."

It was, she insisted, only one country to begin with, before foreigners divided it and allowed the United States to undermine free elections. How can you invade your own country? She wanted people to know that what we were doing in Vietnam didn't make sense. By turning her attention to this issue and being willing to set aside her own career to spread the truth as she understood it, Jane made many enemies as well as many friends. She sacrificed money and reputation as well as time to help end the war in Vietnam and bring our troops home. These truly are the actions of a winter soldier, who continues fighting on even when the political climate is hostile.

7

ON GOLDEN POND

For a while after their marriage, Jane and Tom lived in Studio City, California, but shortly after the birth of their son, Troy, in July 1973, they moved into a house that Henry Fonda called "that shack." It was a modest two-family house only a block from Santa Monica Beach in the working-class neighborhood of Ocean Park, with "no yard, no garage, no place to park the car."

Jane, Tom, Troy, and Vanessa lived upstairs in five wood-paneled rooms filled with plants and books. They shared this home with a small menagerie, including a German shepherd named Geronimo. (Later, there was also a black Labrador retriever named Taxi; it must have attracted some attention when the dogs were called for supper!) A series of friends helped with the kids when Jane and Tom could not be at home to watch them.

Troy's full name is Troy O'Donovan Garity, born July 7, 1973. Jane and Tom named him Garity (it was Tom's mother's maiden name) so that Troy could have his own identity. It wasn't only the political opposition that continued to swirl around his parents that had them concerned; it was also the baggage of celebrity that goes with having a last name that lets people identify you in terms of your parents rather than yourself.

When he was less than a year old, Troy went with his parents to Hanoi, where they filmed a documentary about life there after the war. *Introduction to the Enemy* was a warm, human film that showed the lives of ordinary people struggling to rebuild their blasted lives and blasted land. Its few screenings drew generally good reviews, but the film was never put into general release and so was not seen by very many people.

After that trip to Hanoi, Jane slowly eased back into doing feature films. Over the years, her attitude toward acting had gone through a number of stages. Back when she'd started, she said, "I ate and dressed and lived acting twenty-four hours a day." Later, when she was touring with her "political vaudeville show," she told a reporter seriously, "The most important thing for me is to combine my politics with my profession."

In fact, for a while she wasn't sure that she wanted to entertain audiences at all because it seemed more important to alleviate the world's suffering. She felt that Hollywood films did not show people and their problems as part of society or portray events as part of history. Instead, most movies treated stories as isolated events and didn't help people understand life. She began turning down many parts that did not seem politically useful.

But, she says, "a lot of people thought I was crazy" for doing that, especially some of her radical friends. They said they had seen too many people with important middle-class skills—doctors, lawyers, and others—who rejected their talents along with their class, even though there is a need for doctors and lawyers. And there's a need for people who can reach mass audiences, they reminded Jane, urging her to continue.

Tom Hayden shared their opinion. When he and Jane had first met, "she was thinking of dropping out of acting because it was irrelevant," he said. "I told her I didn't think she should quit."

Eventually, Jane came around to that view herself. Now, she says, "I don't insist on making 'message' films, but I'm not interested in making films that are pure escapism. I like films that show things in some complexity."

Another reason for continuing to make movies is that salaries have reached enormous levels for stars, and she realized the money could be used to help publicize causes and finance political candidates.

"I have money," she said years later. "I have businesses, [but] I try to watch myself very closely to make sure I'm being honest with myself about why I do what I do. Because there's a point when you just don't need any more. You just don't. You have to ask, 'What are you doing with it?' I know what I'm doing with it."

In 1975, Tom, a Democrat, decided to run for U.S. senator from California. Jane had not really done a major Hollywood film since *Klute*, and funds were so low she was even washing and drying all their own clothes at a local laundromat. Since they were basically out of money, Jane picked a purely commercial project for her next film. It is easy to believe she could identify with the woman she played in *Fun with Dick and Jane*.

This was the story of a young couple who had been living on credit in the suburbs until the husband lost his job and they could no longer keep up the payments. As a result, the couple turned to robbery to make ends meet. This was the first comedy Jane had made in years, and people were delighted. They had forgotten her comic flare. Also, it was the beginning of a new career for her because it was a commercial success, her first since *Klute*.

Jane still continued to be politically active, however, and campaigned with Tom up and down the state. She even got help from her famous father.

"The radicalism of the sixties is becoming the common sense of the seventies," Tom informed voters, pointing out that ideas once considered shocking—for example, the notion that feminists and gays could have any serious political impact—were now considered commonplace, just as Social Security and the forty-hour work week had once been considered dangerously subversive notions and were now a fundamental part of American life.

Despite the hard work he and Jane put in, Tom only won 36.7 percent of the vote. But considering that Tom was a notorious radical and his wife even more controversial and that money to campaign against him had come in from right-wing opponents all across the country, that was better than expected. Opposition also came from some of his old friends in "the movement," who accused him of "selling out" and "going Establishment."

When Jane and Tom founded the IPC, they felt they had been banging on the door of the Establishment for a long time. But at last things were changing. Not only was the war over, but the door they'd been pounding on for so long had opened, and they were going in. A year earlier, President Nixon, weakened by the Watergate scandal, had resigned to avoid being impeached for "high crimes and misdemeanors." After that, it seemed much more possible to work within the system.

Later, looking back on that time, Jane said, "It's not what you're told in school, but this wasn't some kind of hippy-dippy movement that kind of rose and fell. Basically, the movement succeeded. We were one of the major currents that led to ending the war. And I think that's the biggest lesson to be learned. We won! We got people elected to office—young people who never could have been elected. There was a new climate in the country that we took advantage of and that we helped spawn."

From the IPC to Tom's own first campaign for elected office was not such a large step when you consider that he had long believed in working from within and had only been protesting and marching and working outside "the system" when there was no alternative available. After running for the Senate, he took these ideas further and in 1977 created the Campaign for Economic Democracy (CED) to work on issues that affect people who do not have full access to political power. Among the people the CED tried to speak for were women, the elderly, blacks and Hispanics, gays, and farm workers. It also promoted rent control and solar energy.

The three main activities of the CED involved getting people interested in politics; influencing the state legislature in Sacramento and the Congress in Washington, D.C.; and trying, through a separate political action committee, to get good people elected to office. At its height, the CED had 12,000 members with a budget of over $1 million per year. It had offices in three cities and by July 1985 had fought election battles in almost two dozen cities and counties. At that point, it began to phase out its local offices and centralize its activities under a new name, Campaign California.

☆ ☆ ☆

In 1975, besides working on Tom's campaign for the U.S. Senate primary, Jane visited the Soviet Union for the first time since she and Vadim had gone there more than a decade earlier. Relations between the United States and the Soviet Union had improved, and as part of the new policy of "detente," the two countries were involved in making a film together. Based on a 1908 play by Maurice Maeterlinck, *The Blue Bird* had first been performed at the Moscow Art Theater under the direction of Konstantin Stanislavsky, the man who invented "the Method." Intended to be a happy children's fantasy, it turned out to be one of the most expensive flops of all time.

Despite the presence of such stars as Jane Fonda, Elizabeth Taylor, and Cicely Tyson, as well as George Cukor's direction, this cooperative attempt at filmmaking was called "sluggish," "a disaster," and "one of the genuine curiosities of all time." Critics were divided over Jane's performance as Night, with one calling it "brilliant" and another critic saying it was "an embarrassment," but audiences didn't bother to find out for themselves.

However, Jane got a lot out of her stay in Russia. The government welcomed her warmly, and one Soviet magazine commented, "She is eager to learn about our country and cement relationships between the two peoples." That was true, but what she learned was not what they expected.

After two months in Leningrad, just before she was going to leave the country, Jane was standing alone in the middle of the street with the tourist guide who had been assigned to her by the government. Suddenly, the guide turned to her and said, "I'm Jewish." She told Jane what that meant in a country where Jews are isolated in many ways. In the Soviet Union, she said, there is institutionalized, state-supported anti-Semitism, and except for isolated cases, it is almost impossible for a Jew to rise to the top of Soviet society.

Standing in the street where she could not be overheard or recorded, the translator shook with emotion as she confided in Jane. Jane remembered this encounter four years later when she visited Israel and learned about a woman named Ida Nudel, who was called the "Guardian Angel of the Prisoners of Conscience" in the Soviet Union.

Whenever anyone was sent to Siberia, for example, Ida would find out somehow and send them food, warm clothes, and letters of support. As long ago as 1971 Ida had applied for an exit visa so that she could move to Israel, but her request was denied. After years of waiting, she hung a banner out of the window of her Moscow apartment. It read "KGB—Give Me My Visa." Soon after, she was arrested by the KGB (the secret police) on a charge of "malicious hooliganism."

Sentenced to four years of hard labor, Ida was the only woman in an all-male prison camp in Siberia, where she was forced to drain swamps, working side by side with hardened criminals. When she returned to Moscow after being released, Ida showed that her spirit was unbroken by immediately holding a press conference.

When Jane heard this story, she began sending letters to government officials in both the United States and the Soviet Union. One year she participated in a marathon while wearing a

T-shirt that said "Running for Ida Nudel." But most of all, she did not forget. The two women corresponded, and sometimes Jane was even able to telephone her. In 1984, Jane arranged a visit to see Ida in the tiny village of Bendery in the southwestern part of the USSR near the Black Sea, where the KGB kept her under close observation.

"If you don't want me to go, let her out," Jane told Soviet officials when they resisted her visit. Even though many of Jane's letters and telegrams to Ida were not delivered, the two did meet and Jane spent Ida's fifty-third birthday with her at Ida's small stucco cottage. Jane calls Ida "the most courageous woman I ever met."

As a result of this visit and the efforts of Jane and many others, the problems faced by Soviet Jews are better known, and in some cases the situation has improved. Worldwide efforts on behalf of Soviet Jews have had an impact on the Soviet policy of *glasnost* (openness) and have led to many changes in the situation, which continues to evolve.

Jane worked on Ida's behalf for three and a half years after meeting with her, and she enlisted the support of other prominent Americans on Ida's behalf. She also spoke out publicly around the country against the abuse of human rights in the Soviet Union.

Finally, in October 1987, on the eve of the summit conference in Washington between President Ronald Reagan and Soviet leader Mikhail Gorbachev, Ida was allowed to leave the USSR. Flown from Moscow to Israel on the private jet of industrialist Armand Hammer, she received a tumultuous welcome from the Israeli people. At the foot of the plane when she landed in Tel Aviv were the prime minister, his entire government, and Jane and Tom. "I can't tell you what a marvelous encouragement Jane was to me," Ida Nudel said.

But there are still 350,000 "refuseniks" who are trying to leave the USSR and who face many hardships as a result. "Once you say, 'I want to go,' " Jane explains, "your life is never the same."

Today people sometimes ask Jane why she is involved in this struggle, since she is not Jewish. The question always surprises her. "Nobody ever asked the Jews who marched with Martin Luther King why they were involved," she points out. "Jews have been involved in practically every progressive cause . . . and nobody ever asked them why."

She says she learned from her father that an injustice to one is an injustice to all. He showed her by example, both in his personal life and in the kind of roles he chose, that one should stand up for the underdog.

☆ ☆ ☆

In 1976, Jane campaigned successfully for a role in *Julia,* based on a supposedly true incident in the life of playwright Lillian Hellman. According to the story, Hellman played a key role during the buildup to World War II by smuggling $50,000 to her friend Julia in Berlin as part of an anti-Nazi plot. Jane played Hellman, and appearing in the title role was Vanessa Redgrave, a fine British actress whose family is as well known in England as the Fonda family is in the United States.

"Oh, just to be able to play in scenes with another woman!" Jane said. "It's the first time I've been given a role in which I'm allowed to feel and express friendship for another woman." In this picture, she promised, "People will see a movie about women who think and who care for each other." She was pleased that they were not shown in terms of their relationships with men. They were not falling in love with men—or out of love, for that matter. And they weren't worried about losing men. They were living on their own.

As usual, Jane worked hard to get into her part. In this case, she traveled to Martha's Vineyard on Cape Cod to visit Lillian Hellman. But instead of talking about the movie, they ended up working to save the older woman's cottage from a hurricane. Jane helped batten down storm windows, cut back roses, and take mirrors off the walls. Fortunately, the hurricane changed its course at the last moment, leaving them untouched. Even without talking, however, Jane learned many things about the way Hellman walked and talked and looked at the world; all of it helped in her performance.

For her next picture, Jane worked with Bruce Gilbert, a former activist she had met when he was in charge of the Blue Fairy day-care center in Berkeley, where Vanessa stayed while Jane was working on *Steelyard Blues*. Together they founded IPC Films (now Fonda Films) and went through a long effort to develop a screenplay about Vietnam. They also made a long search for a box-office star to play opposite her. Finally, they decided to use Jon Voight, an actor friend of Jane's from the days of her traveling antiwar shows. Originally chosen to play her husband, he soon talked himself into the part of a crippled Vietnam vet, with Bruce Dern replacing him as the officer married to Jane, who represented the perfect military wife.

The thematic core for the picture, called *Coming Home*, came from the statement made years earlier by Vietnam veteran Ron Kovic, "I've lost my body, but I've gained my mind." Out of that grew a moving story of a military wife who falls in love with a paraplegic, a veteran who had lost the use of his legs in Vietnam. The affair ends when her husband returns from the war, but the husband is still unable to adjust to daily life at home and eventually becomes yet another victim of the war by taking his own life.

Coming Home took a long time to develop, and during work on it, Jane had already signed a contract to do another picture. That meant only a limited amount of time was available for the actual shooting of this one before Jane had to start on the next. As a result, some key scenes were still missing from the script. Jane asked director Hal Ashby, "Have you ever started a film knowing no more about what we're going to do than this?"

"No," he said.

"I hope it works," she said, grinning.

And it did work, though at least one important scene was simply made up by the original actors, all sitting around a tape recorder and improvising. Later, what they said was written down and polished by a scriptwriter.

The U.S. government did not want to help make this picture. The Veterans Administration would not allow one of its hospitals to be used during the filming, and the army, navy, air force, marines, and National Guard all refused to cooperate. But when the picture was finished, it was shown to a member of the President's Committee on Employment of the Handicapped. She called it "a very important film," the first one she had seen that showed a person who was physically disabled but still a complete human being.

Surely the film's toughest audience was the one that was granted a special preview a few weeks before it opened. That audience consisted of disabled veterans, many of whom entered the private screening with a grudge against Jane for her antiwar efforts. When it was over, several of them were near tears.

Not only was the film a major hit with both audiences and critics in 1978, it also won Oscars for the writers, for Voight, and for Jane—her second as best actress. Not only was her acceptance speech touching, she created an additional response by rendering it in American Sign Language as she spoke, as "my way of acknowledging over fourteen million Americans who are deaf." Also emotional was Voight's speech. With tears in his eyes, he thanked Jane, "whose great dignity as a human being is very moving to me."

Fonda's work on behalf of Vietnam veterans did not end with this movie, however. She has continued to publicize their physical and emotional problems and their need for the nation to do something to help. By dramatically calling attention to those problems, *Coming Home* performed a real service.

As much as any of her later successes, *Coming Home*

proved Jane's contention that "it's possible to say responsible things in movies and still be entertaining." It also set the pattern for many other IPC releases, which tend to show, in her words, "fairly traditional, not particularly courageous women being able to change." In many IPC films, such a woman—an ordinary, good-hearted person—is caught up in events that force her to become more aware of injustice and then stands up to it. Jane's feeling is that by following someone much like themselves, audience members become more informed.

"The more you can relax the tensions of people and make people realize the commonalities instead of the differences, the easier it is for people to accept change," she once said. "Very often people can only open their hearts and minds to new ideas if it's done gently. People can change. As long as I believe that, anything is possible."

☆ ☆ ☆

Comes a Horseman and *California Suite,* Jane's next two pictures, were not highly political, but they did make a lot of money, and they earned her two more Oscar nominations. The first was about a Montana rancher (Jane) trying to hold on to her property in the face of a land grab by a crooked businessman. The second was based on a successful Broadway comedy by Neil Simon. It wasn't very liberated in its attitudes, but Jane enjoyed the discipline and the professional challenge of playing someone she disliked.

And then—pay dirt! Jane and her partner, Bruce Gilbert, developed a story about a television reporter who discovers first-hand the very real ecological dangers of nuclear power. Working with actor/producer Michael Douglas, who provided the original story, they created a role—a television reporter—for Jane to play. Naturally, the nuclear-power industry would not cooperate, so shooting took place at a gas-burning plant that looked a lot like an actual nuclear installation.

But even there, once the movie's theme became known, angry workers shouted, "Go home, you pinko." (Ironically, the

Soviet government has been a major supporter of nuclear power.) Undeterred, Jane continued work on *The China Syndrome*. The name half-jokingly refers to what would supposedly happen if an uncontrolled chain reaction starts inside an atomic reactor and fuses the fuel rods together into a lump in the core—a meltdown. It would burn a hole straight through the earth "all the way to China." Designed to be a simple thriller, the picture was condemned by some supporters of nuclear power, who said the whole idea was "obvious claptrap."

In fact, power companies sent out 400 letters to film critics all over the United States telling them that the picture was coming out and warning that it was filled with lies and inaccuracies. They said it was propaganda and would alarm people unnecessarily. Then, on March 28, 1979—just two and a half weeks after *The China Syndrome* was released—there was a core meltdown at the Three Mile Island nuclear plant near Harrisburg, Pennsylvania. A hole didn't burn through to the other side of the earth, but the fuel rods fused, and radioactive material was released into the surrounding community.

After that, industry critics shut up. The producers canceled advertisements for the film so they wouldn't seem to be exploiting the real-life tragedy. Even without ads, however, audiences flocked to *The China Syndrome* to enjoy an exciting picture and to gasp over lines like the one warning that a meltdown might contaminate "an area the size of Pennsylvania."

This time Jane's preparation for her performance had included hours of work covering real news stories with genuine TV newswomen in Los Angeles. And the effort paid off. *Time's* reviewer said Jane was "truly at the peak of her talent," and she was nominated for an Oscar for the fifth time. Besides delighting critics, the picture was a financial success. It cost $4.2 million to make and had sold $6 million worth of tickets in a matter of days.

But while *The China Syndrome* enhanced Jane's credibility as a box-office star, it did not silence her critics. Soon after it came out, she was on a speaking tour that got picketed by members of the American Legion, an organization of older veterans. She responded by defending herself vigorously.

"I consider myself a good American," Jane said. "My ancestors' home was burned by the British two hundred years ago. . . . I got angry during the Vietnam War, and I've been angry ever since." She might have explained that one of those ancestors, Peggy Fonda, rebuilt a burned-down grist mill with her own hands in order to provide flour to General Washington's army.

More political criticism surfaced that August when California Governor Jerry Brown nominated Jane for a position on the state arts council, an advisory group set up to help the state fund and promote the arts. Although her years in the entertainment community obviously qualified Jane, the state senate rejected her, with many senators condemning her antiwar activities from years before. Brown criticized the senators for this decision, saying they had "behaved like a bunch of little kids."

A few years later, Jane looked back on her activities in the sixties and reflected. "Those were rough, controversial, polarized times—for everyone. I made a lot of mistakes on a lot of different levels in the way I spoke, how I tried to reach people, things like that. I've also grown more patient and, I hope, more understanding." Nevertheless, she admitted that "there's a certain portion of those people who will never forgive me. Never."

On another occasion, she divided her critics into two categories. "One category includes the men who fought the war, and their families. Their sacrifice was noble, even though the war was wrong, and I totally sympathize with their hostility. But I do not forgive the right-wing politicians who sent out mass mailings, saying, 'We must stop the forces represented by Jane Fonda.' They raise millions of dollars by making me into a monster without taking into account that I was acting in the sincere belief that what I was doing, however drastic and non-diplomatic, would help end the war."

And her opinion has not changed today. "There is no

question in my mind that those of us who participated in the antiwar movement were responsible for saving untold numbers of lives by ending the war earlier than it would have ended if it had been left up to our government," she says.

Ecological issues turned up again in Jane's next picture, though *The Electric Horseman* was not nearly as political as *The China Syndrome*. Once again Jane played a reporter, and once again she was matched with Robert Redford. These were the top box-office stars in the country in 1979, so it's not surprising that the picture set a record for making money during its first week of release.

The story concerns a rodeo star (Redford) who now sells breakfast cereal for a living. When he steals a horse and rides it into the wilderness to be released, a TV reporter (Jane) follows him. If that doesn't sound like much, it isn't. But the picture did mark singer Willie Nelson's acting debut. Since the Country Music Association had just named him Entertainer of the Year, his presence didn't exactly hurt the movie's appeal.

Making the film was more difficult than the audience probably realized. For one thing, it was shot on location in Utah, where a series of storms interrupted the filming. On top of that, some scenes were unusually hard to get right. In one case, a simple kiss, the scene had to be shot forty-eight times. That meant poor Jane had to kiss Robert Redford forty-eight times. Of course, it wasn't any easier for him.

Jane's next picture was inspired by stories she had heard from friends in the antiwar movement who had gone on to unionize secretaries. Made by her own IPC Films, *Nine to Five* was named after a Boston-based organization fighting for secretaries' rights. The picture, directed by Colin Higgins, is a hilarious look at the lives and grievances of women in a modern office.

Not only did it have a strong feminist theme; it also allowed Jane to draw on the period years before when she had been the secretary for a Broadway producer. For further firsthand research, she and Bruce Gilbert visited the headquarters of the National Association of Office Workers, in Cleveland, Ohio. In a meeting with about forty women secretaries, Jane asked whether any of the women had ever had fantasies about getting even with their bosses and, according to Bruce Gilbert, "it was like opening a floodgate. Suddenly the most bizarre and funny stories started to come out, and it certainly reinforced our decision to do the film as a comedy."

In the movie, Jane's office escapades with Lily Tomlin and Dolly Parton are something to behold. It was Parton's first appearance on the big screen, and she was an instant hit. So was the picture, which brought in $6 million in theaters alone. Audiences especially loved the elaborate fantasies the women had about getting revenge on their thoroughly hateful boss. After that came the film that is probably going to remain IPC's most beloved presentation.

On Golden Pond was the only picture Jane and her father ever made together, and it is seen with misty eyes by any woman who has ever longed to feel loved and appreciated by her father. "I'm not a religious man," Henry said later, "but I thank God every morning that I lived long enough to play that role."

The story is a simple one about a cranky old man and his wife spending their traditional vacation at their cottage on Golden Pond. Both are aging, and he has a bad heart, so they know this may be their last summer together. In the course of this time, near the end of his life, the man makes friends with a thirteen-year-old boy (played by Doug McKeon) and becomes reconciled with his daughter after a long separation.

It is a touching, heartwarming, and very human story. Henry, of course, was the father; Jane had bought the property so she could make the movie with him. For all the acclaim and even reverence Henry had evoked so far as an actor, the only Oscar he had received was a special "Lifetime Achievement Award." By bringing him the 1981 Academy Award for best actor, this performance put a triumphant cap to his long and distinguished career.

On Golden Pond also won an Oscar for Katharine Hepburn, who played his wife. One of the leading stars of stage and screen for fifty years, Hepburn was very much a legend in her own right. But somehow the two great performers had never worked together, even though they had long admired one another. In fact, Hepburn hadn't even been seen in a new movie for five years.

When the two met, Hepburn looked Henry in the eye and told him frankly, "Well, it's about time." Their first day on the set she gave him a battered old hat that had belonged to Spencer Tracy, a famous actor she had known and loved. Henry wore that hat throughout the picture.

The scenes between Henry and his daughter also attracted audiences. This was the first time he and Jane had worked together since they had been on stage at the beginning of her career. Even though they had made up their personal differences long before, it seemed to moviegoers that the story of a father and daughter coming to terms with each other and finally having the courage to confess their love was close to the real-life story of the Fondas themselves.

"They were playing out scenes from their own turbulent biography, drawing on memories, rather than experience, to give performances worth a crate full of Oscars," said Afdera Fonda after she had seen the movie. She thought it was funny how much of their own lives together turned up in small ways throughout the picture. The love that glowed between Henry and Jane on-screen surely was a result of the love and respect that existed between them in their lives off-screen and was more than professional technique.

Some of those scenes were extraordinarily painful for the performers. Jane felt she was overacting, and sometimes Henry seemed to let the character take over. His grouchiness in the movie was real, and at least once, when the pressure of working with him became too great for his daughter, Hepburn put her arm around Jane and said, "Don't worry, Spencer used to do that to me all the time."

The hardest scene Jane and Henry had to film was the one in which their two characters make peace with one another at last. Reading the script together around the dining-room table, when Jane came to the line where she asks her father to be her friend, both were in tears. When they performed the scene in front of the camera, many of the crew were in tears, too.

The movie was filmed at Squam Lake, near Laconia, New Hampshire, in the summer of 1980. It was a wonderful, close time for all those involved. Jane's seven-year-old son, Troy, even got into the act. He made his film debut—and earned thirty dollars—by fishing off a pier in one of the scenes. The family feeling was bolstered by early-morning exercise sessions for all members of the cast and crew who wanted to join in. The sessions were led by Jane, who had started teaching aerobics at her own workout studio the year before.

Since all the performers were a little in awe of one another, each worked hard to do his or her best. Hepburn looked at Jane as being much like herself at the same age. And Jane idolized the older woman: "The kind of person that young people are never bored by," she once said admiringly. She hated cold water, but her desire to have Hepburn's affection and respect led Jane to the physical test of mastering a backward dive and to her realization of how good it feels to meet such a challenge.

On Golden Pond was Henry Fonda's last movie. Like the character he played in it, he died of heart failure, breathing his last on August 12, 1982, at the age of seventy-seven. Jane stayed with him during his final illness. It was only toward the end of her father's life that she was able to tell him how much he had hurt her and how much she loved him. Afterward, she set aside a period of time for mourning to come to terms with him, with his death, and with her own life.

"I wasn't going to rush it," she said. "I wasn't going to deny it. I wasn't going to sweep it under the rug and deny myself this experience of that process, really thinking about what I had lost." Jane hadn't been able to say a proper good-bye to her mother, and she wasn't going to let that happen again, even if it was painful.

What she learned was that death is an inevitable and natural part of life. And by accepting that, she was able to think about what is important in life. Her father's death made her ask questions. Have I said everything that needs to be said? If not, why not? The larger question she asked is "How can we live our lives so that we can express these important, personal things to the people around us during the healthy part of our lives?"

She also discovered that what really frightened her was the "what ifs" and "if onlys" of life—the "if only I had been a better person" kind of thing. And it dawned on her that life is "not a rehearsal. This is it, here, with our children and our mothers and fathers and lovers and loved ones. Priorities suddenly start to loom. What is really important?"

There were two days of television commentaries and miniature biographies after Henry Fonda died, and Jane watched them all.

"It was a strange experience, watching the nation eulogize my father like a national hero," she reflected, "because to me, he was just a father, and rather a flawed one at that. And during those days, I had to try to sort out for myself who it was I was mourning and how I felt about the fact that he was considered a hero when he had not been all the things I wanted from a father.

"And what I realized was that you can't be all things to all people. People need heroes and legends, and for some reason that's not so easy to understand or explain, my father fulfilled a need for a certain kind of hero. It doesn't matter, really, that he was not perfect. Maybe that's some people's role in life—to be a role model and a hero. And I guess I was able to forgive him then.

"I was so grateful that before he died I had been able to say to him that I forgave him for not being perfect, that he was good enough, that I was grateful for all the things he had given me. And that it didn't really matter that he never responded. I realized how important it is to express your feelings to the people you love, because you never know when you might lose them."

"I rebelled against Father because I needed my own identity," she once summarized. "Then I came close to him again. Then came the Vietnam War, and the particular methods by which I chose to oppose it were foreign to him, so there was tension for about three years. Then he turned against the war and joined me in my efforts. . . . By that time I had my own children and realized that no one's perfect, and all you can do is your best."

Perhaps Jane was helped in these reflections by noticing that she was growing older as well. But unlike many actresses, she did not pretend it wasn't happening. While she hardly noticed the transition from one decade to the next, it did make her resolve more than ever to take better care of herself.

8

JANE FONDA'S WORKOUT

Jane had taken ballet lessons ever since she had first started to be an actress. While working on *They Shoot Horses, Don't They?*, Jane had joined the professional dancers in stretching exercises before beginning work each day and sometimes advised the other actors on how to avoid injury during the grueling shoot. "I could see how knowledgeable she was about dance and about the human body and its parts," one of them recalled. And after a hard day of work on *Julia*, Jane went to exercise classes to unwind.

Things changed when Jane was injured while filming a scene at the end of *The China Syndrome*. She and Michael Douglas were running to board a helicopter and she fell, breaking her foot. That meant she could no longer do her dance classes. Even worse, she was supposed to begin shooting *California Suite* in two months and would have only three weeks to get into shape after her cast came off. Shirlee Fonda took her to an exercise class, and Jane worked out for an hour and a half once or twice a day until she was in shape again.

By the time she worked on *The Electric Horseman*, Jane was exercising regularly. But on location in St. George, Utah, there were no exercise classes of the kind she had come to rely on. Since she hated to exercise alone, Jane asked the managers of a small nearby gym whether they would allow her to conduct a morning workout. She said she didn't want pay, just company.

For six weeks, Jane got her wish. Men from the film crew, high school girls, housewives, even a sixty-year-old woman, took part. Much to her surprise, Jane saw them become obviously healthier. Some members of the group stopped using medication. Women reported they no longer had menstrual cramps. And she found people developed a more positive attitude about themselves, too.

"They felt better about themselves, held their heads higher, and looked more comfortable in their bodies," Jane said. "I decided I wanted to offer the benefits of this kind of workout to more people. I opened my first Workout studio about a year later."

Jane had already been looking for something that would allow her to make a lot of money—not for herself so much as for the causes she believed in. When she saw the results of her exercise class, it became obvious what business she could go into.

Jane Fonda's Workout studio opened in Beverly Hills in 1979. But Jane's real business success came with the exercise book she wrote in 1981 and the 1982 exercise videotape she prepared for home use. It was in *Jane Fonda's Workout Book* that she first confessed to her bulimia and the terrible things she had done to her body for so many years.

"It was the first time that I had ever said that I had the problem," she said. Until then, she had never spoken about it at all. "Not to anyone. Not to my husband, not to anyone." It was only when she was thirty and pregnant for the first time that she began to change the way she treated herself. "As the baby grew inside me, I began to realize my body needed to be listened to and strengthened, not ignored and weakened."

It was not until she was married to Tom and pregnant with Troy that she finally decided to put an end to the years of agony that afflicted her between the ages of seventeen and thirty-five.

During all those years she had continued to stuff herself with food and then vomit, often five to ten times a day.

"Bulimia is an illness," she warns in *Jane Fonda's New Workout and Weight Loss Program*, "just as alcoholism is an illness. It may begin as a device to keep you from gaining weight and seem innocuous enough at first. Like alcoholism, however, it takes on a life of its own, consuming you until your life is out of control. . . ."

"It is usually advisable for anyone suffering from bulimia to seek professional help. Remember, this is a serious, complex disease. While most bulimics can recover, the recovery is not something best attempted alone. Remember, too, that, like alcoholism, bulimia is progressive. The longer it is allowed to continue, the worse the illness becomes, and the harder it is to treat."

Her advice to bulimics is "Tell the people close to you right away. This step—making it harder for you to get away with your covert behavior—can be your first step toward stopping. It may also provide you with the support you need in finding help. If you suspect bulimia in someone you care about, confront the person and encourage him or her to seek treatment. Remind whoever it is—your friend, your child, your partner, yourself— that bulimia is an illness. Bulimia doesn't make them, or you, a weak or bad person."

Jane thinks that eating disorders come from an attempt to take control. "People who want to be perfect, people who feel bad about themselves" and feel that on some deep level their lives are out of control, "may be able to use exercise as a substitute for bingeing and vomiting, and through that, regain control."

"Looks aren't what matters," Jane has learned. "It's how you feel about yourself that matters, and what you do and what you believe in." Perhaps it is those feelings that have helped her age so gracefully, to resist the pressure to be thinner and thinner and to focus on being healthy instead. Many people think of Jane as slender and beautiful, but that attractive figure is a side effect of focusing on regular exercise and proper diet, not the result of unhealthy and self-destructive eating patterns and an obsession with being thin.

"I found that when I was younger," she said once, "looks were all I had. So if I looked terrible, then it was a disaster. Whereas there is so much more when you are older. There's a rich inner life. There's a wider circle of friends. There are pastimes and pleasures that one has discovered over the years."

As time went on, Jane began making a conscious effort to play women who were her own age so that people could have a chance to see a woman deal openly with growing older.

"I think when you pass forty," she said, "you automatically start thinking about your mortality. There's no question about it. People you know die more frequently. Friends begin to slip away. Parents are getting older. It's the second half of your life, and you can start thinking about what you want to do with it, how you can make it more meaningful. It's not negative to be aware of mortality.

"When you're younger, you don't know what's what. You don't know what's your responsibility, your fault, and so you tend to blame other people when things go wrong. As you get older, you begin to realize that a lot of the things that happen to you are your own fault and that the things that happen to you over and over again have something to do with you. Then you realize that you can't cop out anymore by blaming someone else."

A few months after Henry Fonda's death, Tom Hayden had been elected to the California State Assembly from the 44th District (West Los Angeles). Because right-wing opponents from all over the United States contributed money to defeat him, the race cost Tom over one and a half million dollars. Almost half of that money came from Jane, who was infuriated that people living thousands of miles away should try to decide the outcome of a local race. She vowed to fight financial pressure with financial pressure and promised never to be outspent if money was what was required in order to ensure a fair race.

"I think the Republicans knew," says Jane, "and anyone looking at Tom's history would know, that he is an excellent organizer and an achiever. I think the Republicans felt they'd better cut him off at the pass, keep him from ever getting in. And that's why the money was spent. They don't count on someone like Tom having access to that kind of money."

Without that kind of support, she said, "it would have meant that the only people who can be elected are the people who never do anything brave and courageous and risk taking." She points out that Martin Luther King is a legend now but was attacked by the government during his lifetime, spied on by the FBI, and maligned as a Communist and for being "un-American." Similarly, Jane says, "the people who founded this country—Tom Paine, for example—were accused of being dangerous radicals."

"I feel really strongly that it's important for young people not to be discouraged from being idealistic and from being brave, even if it means being controversial. If it had been impossible for Tom to be elected, it would have sent a signal of despair."

During the election, Tom jokingly told reporters, "This district has the widest gap in income of any in the United States—that's between me and my wife's." In 1976, Jane said that she would be speaking out for Hayden even if she were not married to him because "I believe in his program." She spent four hours a day, five days a week, campaigning for him, too, knocking on the doors of over eight hundred buildings to talk with voters about the candidates and issues.

Unlike many of his old radical friends, Tom had not disappeared from politics. He had taught history at two Los Angeles colleges, wrote several books, and (partly because he married Jane) was even able to enter mainstream American politics successfully. His unsuccessful first campaign, for U.S. Senate in 1976, gave him credibility. After that, serving in several appointed positions for California governor Jerry Brown and years of work for the CED helped his second campaign—his first for a state assembly seat—achieve success.

Still, political opposition continued. Jane and Tom's former enemies and members of the diehard right have continued to fight them both. As recently as the summer of 1986, a member of the Assembly tried to have Tom thrown out of office because of his opposition to the Vietnam War two decades earlier.

Because of such pressures on Tom and other progressive candidates, Jane made a deliberate decision to pour the profits from her exercise business into the CED.

☆ ☆ ☆

As a young actress, Jane told interviewers that she preferred frozen foods. "My refrigerator looks like a supply station at the South Pole" was the way she once put it. All that changed when she went on a health kick. During that phase, birthday cakes were heavy bricks of organic everything, topped with a few strawberries. Before long, however, she had adjusted. And no one seemed to mind if she sneaked a little wheat germ into her recipes. The children could still "pig out" for days on Halloween candy.

"Birthdays [at our house] are sugary celebrations of gooey frosted cakes and ice cream just like everyone else's," she admits. But she doesn't keep soda pop or candy around the house. Sweets are an exception to the normal routine, though that doesn't mean you can never find a cookie in her kitchen.

Today salt and butter are not much used by the Haydens, and Jane takes vitamin and mineral supplements daily. But while she eats a lot of grains and fresh fruit and vegetables, she's not a vegetarian. She has cut back on meat, and red meat in particular, but still splurges sometimes on a hamburger with everything.

"I used to skip breakfast in the days of binge and fast, feast and famine," she wrote. "My mornings were half as efficient as they are now because I'd get tired. I was irritable, and I couldn't concentrate well." Today breakfast might be a bowl of yogurt and half a banana, strawberries from her garden, or a healthy cereal like shredded wheat.

The video, *Jane Fonda's Workout*, stayed on top of the sales charts for three years, selling thirty times the number of copies of an average successful video. By 1985, she had set a record by having three videos in the Top Ten—*Jane Fonda's Workout*, *Prime Time Workout*, and *Workout Challenge*. In the fall of 1986, her *Low Impact Workout* also soared to the top of the charts quickly and stayed there for months. The *StartUp* video in 1988 and the *Complete Workout* video in 1989 were no exceptions.

The first *Workout* video had sold a million copies by the end of 1985, and the other two had sold 200,000 each. More titles have already been prepared for later release. And the *Workout* book was also a success. It stayed on the publishing industry's Top Ten list for ninety weeks and sold 2 million copies in hardcover. But long before it had gone into twenty printings it, too, set a record. Slightly over a year after it was first published, the book produced a royalty check for $3 million—the largest single payment ever made to an author for sales of a book.

The success of her exercise business took Jane very much by surprise. "As it began to evolve, it took on a life of its own," she said. "I began to want to make it as useful a business as I could. I never at any point along the way expected it to take off the way it did." But that didn't mean she was changing careers. "I have turned something that was a daily concern of mine for twenty-five years—fitness—into an incredibly successful business. But I am not a businesswoman, I'm still an actress."

Even though there is a joke that the real way Jane stays in shape is by lugging bags of money to the bank, she has not been the primary beneficiary from the *Workout*. The four books, five videos, the studios, and an assortment of audio records and cassettes were all owned by Campaign California until 1984, when Jane bought them back again. For five years the proceeds provided the group with an income of as much as $500,000 annually—half of its budget. Some of the money also goes to a children's camp that she and Tom started.

Much of the money Jane raises from the *Workout* goes to issue campaigns, not to specific candidates for office. The reason is that she does not feel she can ask Republicans to do aerobic exercises with her and then give the money to Democratic candidates.

"Most of the women who come to my studio," she says, "believe in women's rights, don't like nuclear energy, don't like hazardous-waste dumping. They're with me on the issues that we work to correct." She insists that "money's not evil. It's how you use it that's sometimes a problem."

The other thing that she and Tom have done with the *Workout* money is to buy a 118-acre ranch on a mountaintop above Santa Barbara, California. Lying about seventy-five miles from former president Ronald Reagan's Western White House, the sprawling retreat is located in the Los Padres National Forest in the Santa Ynez Mountains and overlooks the Pacific Ocean. In Jane's words, "It's very, very beautiful."

There are two wood-burning stoves and a windmill to generate electricity for the one-story frame cottage where Jane's family would stay when they can get away. The cottage also has a small fireplace and a cluttered porch filled with baseball equipment and fishing gear. The screen door is scratched by three dogs, and inside all is cozy. The rustic kitchen has pine cabinets, and Jane enjoys washing dishes and cleaning house. The building is an old one, though. When she and Tom went to insulate it, they found the walls stuffed with newspapers dating back to 1905.

Tom kept a seventeen-foot boat up there for bass fishing on Lake Cachuma. Jane sometimes went with him, but more often stayed behind wondering, "What does a smallmouth bass have that I don't?" The real reason they bought the ranch, however, was not for their own pleasure but to operate it as a summer camp for children. Each year, fifty kids at a time come for two-week sessions at Laurel Springs Camp. They come from all economic, cultural, and social classes to experience living together. Half of the camp's energy comes from a wind generator, and the main lodge is solar heated. Other facilities include a children's theater that is an important part of the camp's program, which teaches self-awareness through participation in the arts.

"Through the performing arts, children learn a lot about trusting, cooperation, and self-esteem," Jane says. "They learn a lot about themselves. We send the older kids out white-water rafting and rock climbing. It's an amazing experience." Children choose among drama, comedy, improvisation, dance, song and music, arts and crafts, photography, and video.

"We don't train them to become professional little actors and actresses," Jane says. "We use the performing arts to train kids in trust and self-confidence in working with others."

The camp is not inexpensive, even though the fees cover only about 40 percent of the cost. Many of the children do not pay at all.

"I just wanted to create an opportunity for kids to realize a little paradise in their lives and have an adventure in really building a better place," Jane says. "You know how segregated our society is, along all kinds of lines. Here you have kids from ghettos, children of farm workers, kids of movie stars. They're all thrown together in the same swimming pool."

She and Tom have spent a lot of time at the camp and Troy goes up each summer, although Vanessa stopped when she was eighteen. Jane worked out daily with some of the kids, but not with Tom, who found that type of exercise boring, though he also loves the camp. After all, this is the man who once said, "My only regret in life is that I didn't have ten more kids."

"I worked in camps when I was a kid," Tom comments. "But in addition to that, I have always been involved in kids' programs—including setting up voluntary child-care programs wherever I've lived. . . . I love kids. I guess I didn't have the money to do anything really significant for kids until now."

One day at the camp, Jane mentioned that she was forty-five years old, and the kids told her that she should not reveal her age. She thought of the reply made by feminist Gloria Steinem when someone told her, "You don't look forty-five." Steinem said, "This is what forty-five looks like."

Jane thought to herself, I wouldn't want to go back to their ages, and she feels most women her age would agree. "I know myself better now," she says. "If something goes wrong, I know when I can blame myself for it and when I can blame somebody else." When you're young, she says, you just stumble around without anything to compare anything to. "You don't really know what you want out of a relationship, and you don't know the difference between sex and love, and I wouldn't want to go back for anything. I was miserable until I was well into middle age, and I don't think I'm unique."

Also, looking ahead, she notes that younger women are having fewer children and that women live longer than men. As a result, older women are becoming a greater portion of the population of the country. "By the year 2000," she points out, "older women will be the largest portion of American society. Our potential impact on the marketplace, on politics, on society as a whole, is quite staggering.

"Besides, what's bad about aging, except that our culture is geared to youth? Aging is not a disease. Wrinkles and the loss of elasticity in skin is not a disease. It's a reality." Other realities are that two-thirds of the women over sixty-five live alone and two out of three adults who live in poverty are women. Obviously something needs to be done about that. And it isn't necessarily a matter of money.

Sometimes just loving care can make a big difference. For the last two years of her life, Tom's mother lived with her son and his family. "When she first came to us from Wisconsin," Jane said, "everyone thought she was senile. There were all the indications that she had had strokes and was senile. But after she had been with us for three weeks, the stimulation of being with people and having people talk to her and give her three square meals a day changed everything. . . . She was just lonely and inactive. She was rusting."

If Tom's mother had moved in with them when he and Jane were first married, their little upstairs residence would have been pretty crowded, but after almost a decade in the house by the beach, Jane and Tom had moved into a $1 million solar-heated house in a wealthy, more conservative neighborhood. Despite the price, the home is hardly spectacular, and is surprisingly modest by movie-star standards. Jane still has a cozy study, but there's no real dining room. Instead, there's an eating area just off the large, airy kitchen. And there's a homey, overgrown flower garden in the front yard.

"To have a house and security has nothing to do with selling out," Jane said a little defensively back in 1984, just after the family moved in. "There's nothing wrong with being comfortable. I wanted it. The kids were getting bigger. The dogs are getting bigger. I wanted privacy. But we make it available to a lot of people as a meeting place, for receptions, as a place to raise money."

Jane and Tom's marriage worked remarkably well for years, and they were able to keep their personal lives private, even though they are both highly independent, tend to challenge the world rather than just accept it, and come from very different backgrounds. Naturally, that took some adjustments.

"When you're married, as I am, to a very powerful, famous woman," Tom once said, "and you've been raised in a male-dominated environment, learning is not so academic. The question is how to live through changes in life-style at full force. You feel your personality being changed, remade. The changes are deep and psychological."

"Like most marriages that last," Jane explains, "there are periods that are intensely romantic, and there are periods when there is less time for romance. The nice thing about being grown-up is that you learn that it's not the end when things are less romantic. In relationships, romance ebbs and flows, but the bedrock of marriage is respect. When we make time to go away together and are reminded of how precious we are to each other, the relationship is romantic again. But it is impossible for people with children and many responsibilities to maintain a constant level of romance."

Since Tom retained some of his bachelor habits long after marriage and Jane has a "cleanliness fetish," they often had to compromise. They are very different people. Jane does the workout regularly, for example, using weights sometimes. Other times, she runs three to four miles in the morning, rides a bike, or swims. On weekends she goes on eight-mile hikes in the Santa Monica Mountains. In contrast, Tom finds programmed exercise "boring" but runs three miles a day, plays baseball regularly, and works out annually with the Los Angeles Dodgers.

Jane loves to cook and has spent hours working on an elaborate meal, only to watch it grow cold because Tom and Troy were playing baseball together and didn't get back on time. In contrast, Tom tends to stir-fry vegetables when he's hungry and then eat standing up.

Each year, they made time for at least one family trip to somewhere like Israel or Japan, and in between there were family outings for sports, movies, and restaurants. Also, there was a lot of entertainment at home, since they rarely went out during the week unless business made it unavoidable. But Jane sometimes has to spend weeks on location making a picture, and late-night sessions of the state legislature are not uncommon for Tom.

Troy, in particular, liked to stay home and follow a regular routine. "I get along with my parents more than a lot of my friends at school," he once said. When the family was at home alone, life was no different than for millions of other families. On a quiet night, Troy was likely to demand that Jane scratch his back. And Vanessa long made a daily ritual of complaining that her father, Roger Vadim, was a better cook than her mother.

Vanessa skipped a grade of school when she was fifteen and still got straight A's. When it came time for college, she insisted on attending Brown University in Rhode Island. Like any mother watching her child move out of the nest, Jane tends to worry. She personally escorted Vanessa to school and helped her pick out her apartment furnishings from local Salvation Army and Goodwill stores, reluctant to let go. She remembered how she responded when she began living on her own, with no one to make her knuckle down at Vassar and really learn.

Eventually, in fact, all the pressures on Jane and Tom became too great, and in mid-February 1989, they announced that they were separating. Although they both kept a resolute silence about their reasons, close friends were not surprised. Tom used to joke that "if Jane and I have an evening at home alone together, it is a scheduling mistake by the staff." Apparently, however, his joke was very close to the truth. Both have busy lives and their careers had been taking them on increasingly divergent paths.

The separation had a number of immediate consequences. Tom moved into a small apartment a few miles away, and they canceled the annual Easter retreat at their ranch. Previously, political writers, activists, and movie stars gathered informally, sang old songs together, and relaxed. Tom would lead the Sunday service, and Jane always dressed as the Easter Bunny.

As this book is being written, there has been an announcement of plans for a divorce. It seems obvious, however, that no matter how hard they try to preserve a dignified silence, both will continue to be public figures, and as such, even their private agonies will be the subject of gossip and speculation.

☆ ☆ ☆

The first chapter of *Jane Fonda's Workout Book* begins with a statement that might have been astonishing to most of her fans: "As a child, I was your basic klutz—awkward, plump, and self-conscious. I was convinced that when God had passed out gracefulness, I had dropped my share. I could hardly get across a room without bumping into something. I resented my body."

If anyone had told Jane that she was only an "ugly duckling" who would one day turn into a swan, she would not have believed it. Now she realizes that the reason she spent so many years addicted to thinness and going through the dangerous cycles of bulimia is that she was thinking of herself as a product, not as a person. "Life is what matters," she says. The truth is, "The glow and energy of the healthy woman is the ultimate beauty, the only beauty that will last."

As the wife of a politician, the mother of two children, and a businesswoman as well as a leading actress, Jane divided her time among many activities. Often she's still so busy that she even has to schedule her free time to make sure she has some. It was deliberate scheduling that used to let her attend Troy's Little League games and to be on hand, for example, when he hit his first home run in a Santa Monica park. It also helped her find the time to be with Vanessa three nights in a row to help her daughter put on makeup for a high school play.

Jane is quick to point out that she has had the help of an office staff, a workout staff, a film-development company, and when her kids were little, someone who could feed them and take them to and from school when she couldn't. Now that Vanessa is a college student, things have changed somewhat. But still, when Vanessa's car broke down in the middle of the night a few years ago, Jane was the one who got up and drove her home. Some of a mother's obligations cannot be delegated.

"It worries me when people say, 'How did you do it all?' Who are you kidding? I'm rich. It's easy for me to do a whole lot, but there are women who do far more than I do, with none of the help—and do it very, very well.

"Look at the women who lost their husbands or were abandoned or divorced, who have one or more children, who are holding down one or more jobs plus putting themselves through school at the same time," Jane demands. "I mean, talk about superwomen. And they do hold down the job, and they do get a degree, and they do raise decent kids. And they don't have staff or secretaries or public relations people. And they never get any credit."

But Jane has been legitimately successful. And she gets more popular all the time. A 1976 *Redbook* poll showed her as one of the 120 most admired women in America. A Field poll three years later in California found that 49 percent of the people surveyed held her in high regard and 45 percent of the people surveyed held her in low regard, with only 6 percent having no opinion. In 1985, the *World Almanac* discovered that Jane was the top heroine of young Americans in grades eight through twelve, and, that April, the Roper poll listed her as the top heroine of young Americans. Yet all of this has left her almost surprisingly modest.

"The polls say I'm very influential, especially among women and among young people," she says. "If that's true, if the polls are accurate, I think it's to the extent that I am quite honest about my weaknesses, about where I've been weak in the past. I try to do this with my kids, too, which is not to set myself on a pedestal.

"I don't pretend to have all the answers, certainly not for anyone's personal life. I'm just trying to figure out how, as an actress, I can responsibly use what money I earn and what fame I have to improve the quality of people's lives."

9

THE DOLLMAKER

In the five years after *On Golden Pond,* Jane only made three films for theatrical release. Of all the IPC pictures, the least successful at the box office was *Rollover,* a high-finance thriller with Kris Kristofferson. It examines the potentially devastating economic consequences if all the Arab oil money on deposit in U.S. banks were to be withdrawn at the same time.

Far more important, however, was Jane's first movie made for television. She made it after seeing *Roots* in January 1977. The eight-part miniseries told the history of an American family from the days when they were slaves to an earlier time when they had been free people in Africa. Because *Roots* was powerful drama as well as wildly popular, Jane and her partner, Bruce Gilbert, decided that television reaches a large enough audience and that it can truly make a difference. "You can't ignore television," she said. "You've got to join it if you're at all interested in communication."

The Dollmaker, in which Jane played a mountain woman named Gertie Nevels, was the fitting culmination of a dream she had had for twelve years. Ever since she first read the Harriet Arnow novel of the same name, Jane had wanted to bring it to life, and she finally decided that television was the best way to do so. On the day after she won her second Oscar, for *Coming Home* in 1979, she had proposed the project to ABC-TV. But even after the network agreed, it took years of effort to translate the story to the screen.

For one thing, the script did not begin to fall into place until 1981, when Bruce Gilbert asked Hume Cronyn to read the book. Cronyn, then playing a banker in *Rollover*, loved it and recommended novelist Jane Cooper to do the writing. She had worked with him on a successful Broadway show called *Foxfire*, which had a somewhat similar setting.

To play the part, Jane first had to become acquainted with the daily lives of the characters involved. She considered the role of Gertie to be "the most challenging I've ever had, a character as far from what I am as I'll ever play." The reason? Gertie was an uneducated Kentucky sharecropper in the Depression years before World War II. She is uprooted from her farm and forced to move into a Detroit housing project, along with her five children, after her husband finds a factory job in the city.

One of the people Jane told about the project was Dolly Parton, her costar in *Nine to Five*. Dolly was from Sevierville, Tennessee. She had been born in a mountain shack and had been raised in a family that not only grew its own food but even made its own soap. Jane considered Dolly "a mountain woman in the truest sense of the word."

When Jane described the story to her, Dolly replied, "Look, there have been so many things done wrong about my people, so much that was stereotyped, that if you're going to do this movie, do it right." After they finished working on their comedy together, Dolly organized a ten-day trip aboard her customized touring bus so that Jane could see parts of the country that few outsiders ever get to know. They traveled through parts of Missouri, Arkansas, Tennessee, and Kentucky, going as far back into the mountains as they could.

"I entered a world that no one I know has ever entered,"

Jane said. "My children will probably never know it—and that's a world as close to that of our early pioneers as possible. Now, that's a world that's dying out."

In 1982 and 1983, Jane returned to that world and lived several weeks with two of the farm families she had met. One farm was in Mount Vernon, Kentucky, which had a population of 2,300, and the other was in Arkansas. She managed to fit in, wearing pigtails when she visited the post office in town and working long, hard hours.

"I especially learned a lot from Lucy and Waco Johnson," she said, referring to the couple she had lived with in the Ozarks. "Lucy is an artist. She makes dolls in addition to working on her farm. I worked really hard with them. I'm in pretty good shape, but I spent one day doing what seventy-four-year-old Waco does every day—chopping wood, milking cows, churning butter— and at the end of the day I couldn't move."

Jane also cooked—dried-apple pie, hoe cakes, and corn- bread. She baked biscuits, too, and dined on 'possum. Since the character of Gertie is an artist, Jane also learned to whittle. She especially treasures the large, beautifully carved apple that she made and displays it prominently in her living room. Not only does it look like an apple; it also has a very realistic bite taken out of it—even though experts told her it would be impossible to carve a real-looking bite.

Today Jane continues to exchange letters with the Johnsons. And in 1985 she joined actresses Sissy Spacek and Jessica Lange in testifying before Congress about the effects of the farm crisis. They had each learned about rural life-styles while making movies and were concerned about the growing hardships faced by this important sector of the American economy.

Another thing Jane learned for *The Dollmaker* was how to speak the dialect of the people she was going to portray. She spoke it from the time she got on the plane to go on location until shooting was finished six weeks later, refusing to drop it even when she was off camera. During phone conversations with her family, she continued to speak with a thick mountain twang that they could hardly understand: "I'm here at the ho-tel," Jane said, demonstrating the accent. "It drove my kids crazy."

Jane put in the extra effort of mountain travel and manual labor to prepare for this picture because she wanted her performance to be especially good. Gertie, she felt, is "somebody trying to be true to herself but almost losing it." Gertie is a woman who combines the simple and the practical. "She's like so many women who don't even realize the artistry of what they do, even if it's just bringing up children, being good wives, taking care of their homes, caring about values. Those things are never raised to a level of importance in our culture, never given their due."

Jane was convinced that Gertie would have been friends with Tom Joad, the Oklahoma farmer played by her father in *The Grapes of Wrath*. Originally, she'd wanted Henry to play Gertie's father in *The Dollmaker*, but he died long before the picture went into production.

"Over the years, I often heard my father say, while being interviewed, that he had been fortunate enough over a period of time to occasionally play a character that was so remarkable that it improved him as a human being. My character, Gertie, does that for me by being an extraordinary woman without knowing it. I don't think I have ever liked a character as much as I have liked her. It was the most fulfilling and happy experience that I've had as an actress in twenty-five years of work."

One of the things Gertie does not know is that her talent for carving dolls is a genuine gift. Throughout much of the story, she is carving a wooden head of Christ that she "can't find a face for." In the end, she has to destroy that sculpture to get the wood she needs for the dolls she has to make and sell in order to leave the city housing project and return to a country farm where she belongs. In some ways, it is a "typical" Fonda role: a woman who becomes a bit independent and learns to believe in herself.

Jane is not in the movie's final scene, but she stood by and watched as it was being filmed. When the last shot was completed, director Daniel Petrie turned to her and said, "Well, Miss Fonda, it's a wrap," meaning that it was wrapped up, finished. "Then Jane reached out and put her arm around me," he said. "And she sobbed for ten minutes. Her whole body was shaking. I think it was because the character was dead and she was in mourning."

It had been a dream for twelve years, and now it was over. "It was the hardest but happiest experience I've ever had as an actress," Jane said. "It was certainly the most challenging. I was scared to death, absolutely terrified, the whole twelve years when I thought about whether I could do it or not. In the end, it was a joy."

The performance won Jane an Emmy to join the two Oscars she had already received.

Less exciting but more successful was *Agnes of God* in 1985, which dealt with the thorny issues of religious faith and scientific skepticism. Jane played Dr. Martha Livingstone, a psychiatrist who believes more in science than in religion. Anne Bancroft, playing the mother superior of a convent, engages Jane in a number of debates that amplify our society's ongoing controversy between faith and reason.

These issues are raised by the title character, Agnes, a young nun played by Meg Tilly. Agnes is a highly religious woman who is subject to visits by angels and to receiving religious signs. She has become pregnant but can't remember having intercourse.

As usual, Jane prepared heavily for her role by seeking actual experience that would be relevant to her character. In this case, she needed to know what psychiatrists do, how they work with patients, and what types of problems people can have. To find out what happens between doctors and patients, Jane visited a Los Angeles psychiatric hospital to view videotapes of a session conducted under hypnosis and watched a live psychiatric session through a two-way mirror.

Jane was pleased to be working with Anne Bancroft. Since Anne had been appearing on Broadway with Henry Fonda during the period in which Jane had decided she wanted to become an actress, Jane was eager to hear Anne reminisce about the experience. Jane learned that once, Henry Fonda had become so worked up during a rehearsal that he slugged someone. Jane was delighted to hear that her father was not always as calm and in control as he seemed at home.

In talking about this film, Jane was often asked about her own beliefs. She replied, "I have always believed in God, though I have no formal religion." Another time she went a step further to explain, "I believe in a benevolent, loving God, and I believe in the power of prayer."

Jane's thirty-fifth film was *The Morning After.* A thriller somewhat like *Klute,* it came out in 1986 and brought Jane her seventh Oscar nomination. In this picture, she plays an actress who has destroyed her career through alcoholism and who is on the run from a murder charge. The movie follows a formula used in many Hollywood classics: The leading lady can't remember anything about the murder, so she is not sure whether she is guilty or innocent. In this case, Jane receives some timely assistance from someone her character calls "a red-necked bigot"—a narrow-minded ex-cop who helps her begin the process of recovery.

This knight in tarnished armor is played by Jeff Bridges, an actor Jane called "an explosion waiting to happen." And with director Sidney Lumet, Jane was again working with someone who had also worked with her father. In fact, Lumet directed 12 *Angry Men,* not only one of Henry's most memorable performances but the only film Henry ever produced himself. Jane had wanted to work with Lumet ever since and threw herself into the *Morning After* part. For research, she attended meetings of Al Anon, an organization for families of alcoholics, and Alcoholics Anonymous.

The biggest film Jane has ever done is *Old Gringo*, an epic filmed partly in the shadows of the ancient Aztec pyramids at Teotihuacan, Mexico. Produced by Fonda Films, *Gringo* began filming in mid-January 1988, though it was not to be released until October 1989. An exciting action adventure that takes place against a vast panorama of mountains and sky, it is filled with the thundering hooves of horses and the battle cries of soldiers. The movie is based on a novel by Carlos Fuentes, a leading Mexican writer.

"I met Carlos Fuentes about ten years ago in Santa Barbara," Jane told an interviewer who had made an expedition to the hot, windy, dusty location in Venta de Cruz where the picture was being made. "Tom introduced us. I told Carlos then that I was interested in doing a project about both of our countries."

She was even more interested when he mentioned an unpublished manuscript, then called *Frontiers*, which eventually became *Old Gringo*, his twelfth novel. The two of them quickly began adapting it for the movies, and Fuentes revised the central character with her in mind. Also starring in the film are Gregory Peck in the title role and Jimmy Smits, best known for his TV performances on "L.A. Law."

Peck, seventy-one years old, plays Ambrose Bierce, a real-life San Francisco newspaperman, critic, and author who disappeared in Mexico in 1913 when he went to join the rebel troops of Pancho Villa. Jane plays the fictional part of Harriet Winslow, an unmarried schoolteacher from the United States who moves to Mexico to teach English, is caught up in the revolution, and has an affair with Smits, who plays a fiery and handsome general in Villa's army.

"When Harriet arrives in Mexico, her body and mind are alienated from one another," Jane said. "The [Mexican] culture initially terrifies her, and she's rejecting it," but eventually she learns "to understand, respect, and love" the differences she finds. Fuentes says that if Harriet were living in today's world, "she'd be Jane Fonda making a film about what she learned in Mexico."

"This isn't an easy movie," Jane said. "I think there's enough passion and sex and excitement and action so the movie will be accessible to the kind of audience I want to reach. And the kind of audience I want to reach aren't people who read very much."

Most of the picture was shot at the Miranda Hacienda, the remains of an eighteenth-century estate that once covered 5,000 acres. Many of the original buildings were reconstructed in detail by the film company, which hired many local residents to help, including 500 carpenters and 150 members of the technical crew. The movie took fifteen weeks to film and lasts over two hours. In one scene, there are 700 extras.

But the most interesting person that was hired in Mexico probably is Samuel Valdez de la Torre, who was discovered when he was a tour guide. After being tested to see how he would look in front of a camera, Sam was put into costume and given the key role of Pedrito, a fourteen-year-old who is caught up in the revolution. His favorite scene is the intensely dramatic last meeting he has with Smits. When it was over, everyone congratulated him and "Even Miss Jane Fonda cried," he said.

Shooting finished in mid-June 1988, but because extra time was needed to get the picture ready for release, it was held from theaters until October 1989. That July, however, long before *Old Gringo* was ready for audiences to see, Jane was deeply involved in a very different picture in New England.

Originally called *Union Street* and then *Letters*, this new project became *Stanley & Iris* by the time it was released in February 1990. It was to have begun in Connecticut in July 1988, with Jane and Robert De Niro starring. A few veterans, however, decided to protest Jane coming to their town. Two town councils in the state even went so far as to vote that they didn't want her to come there.

Although an anti-Jane resolution was defeated eleven to two, protesters led a rally in which she was hanged in effigy. The next day these Vietnam veterans gained additional publicity by spitting at a Catholic priest who opposed their actions. He said that much of the protesters' anger was really directed at what they had experienced in Vietnam and feelings of guilt they harbored about the war. "There's a much bigger issue here, and that's not being discussed," he said. He believed the incident occurred because he was holding a card that said "Forgive." He was worried about what might happen later. "That [attack] was directed at me," he said. "What's going to happen when Jane gets here?"

"And yet," wrote one local newspaper columnist, "if you asked these veterans why they served in Vietnam, they would almost certainly say, 'We were there to preserve democracy, free speech.' "

All the fury, however, on the part of a few, could not completely disguise the fact that most everyone else in the state was thrilled to have a distinguished cast come to film a movie there—especially since the community could expect an income of about $15–$20 million from the project.

Much of this controversy was carried on long before Jane arrived. On her way back from Mexico, she stopped in Los Angeles for not much longer than it took to make her *Complete Workout* video, which is less challenging than some of the early ones but far more sophisticated. Then she headed east. Despite the noisy objections of a few, polls showed that more than three-fourths of the residents wanted Jane to visit. In fact, in mid-July, when extras were being hired, 5,000 people turned out to compete for 500 parts. And although there were a few picketers every day, several hundred people came to applaud Jane the first day she was on the set, and large crowds often came just to watch all the activity.

"I knew that the majority of people wanted us to come, that it would be exciting and good for the local economy," she told reporters a month later. "I also thought it would be a mistake to accept the false proposition that I wasn't wanted here."

Jane was also very conciliatory toward the veterans. She made a point of meeting with them to discuss the Vietnam War and apologize once again for some of the mistakes she had made two decades earlier. One night in August, Jane and De Niro raised $27,000 at a benefit for children suffering from birth defects caused by their father's exposure to Agent Orange, a defoliant widely used in Vietnam by the United States. More than 2,500 came to the barbecue and concert, which were held at a nearby amusement park, and 400 of the visitors waited in line for up to an hour to pay $5 and have their photo taken with the famous pair. Jane just smiled brightly the entire time and kept up a tireless stream of small talk.

The night before, they had raised an additional $10,000 for the Literacy Volunteers of America, because Waterbury had an illiteracy rate of 10 percent. In addition, her slide show on Ida Nudel drew a standing ovation the night she presented it. This round of activity, and her appearance on national television to apologize for having been insensitive in the way she tried to communicate her concerns years before, did much to reconcile many of the veterans and to heal the wounds of the past.

Later that month, filming moved to Toronto, where the picture was delayed when Jane broke her nose—the result of a collision that occurred when she turned a corner while out bicycle riding and ran head-on into another cyclist.

Despite all the controversy involved in making it, *Stanley & Iris* has a story that is hard to dislike. Iris (Jane) works in a bakery factory where she meets Stanley (De Niro) and discovers that he is illiterate. Stanley's true genius is revealed only after she teaches him to read. It's an important subject, and the story is poignant.

After these two important movies, Jane and Lois Bonfiglio,

her partner in Fonda Films, took on a new challenge by helping to produce a movie based on Neil Sheehan's Pulitzer Prize–winning book about the Vietnam War, *A Bright Shining Lie.* Sheehan had been a reporter in Vietnam who was later involved in helping bring to light *The Pentagon Papers.* Jane had found his book dramatically exciting and wanted to be involved in bringing it to the screen, even though there would be no role for her in the movie. The picture is expected to become the first ever produced by Fonda Films in which Jane does not appear.

☆ ☆ ☆

"One of the great things about being an artist," Jane says, "is that you don't have to be diplomatic. You can stir things up. The role of an artist is to be controversial, to shake people up and make them think with new parts of their minds."

Jane does this not only by the movies she makes, but by taking an active role in fund-raising for many different causes. In 1986, for example, she and Tom organized a caravan of young Hollywood stars to campaign for a clean-water initiative sponsored by Campaign California. Judd Nelson, Ally Sheedy, Demi Moore, and Rob Lowe were among those who returned in 1988, again traveling up and down the West Coast to register voters and support the Democratic presidential campaign of Massachusetts governor Michael Dukakis.

During the massive April 9, 1989, march on Washington sponsored by the National Organization of Women (NOW), Jane was one of the celebrities who joined a march and rally of more than a quarter of a million people demanding that the Supreme Court uphold its 1973 *Roe v. Wade* decision granting women the right to safe, legal abortions.

Just as Jane publicly fought for issues, in a public way she has worked out the legacy of a childhood spent amid fame and luxury in Hollywood and New England. In doing so, she has come a long way from the little girl who acted like a boy to get her father's attention, the teenager who thought she was an ugly klutz, and the bulimic model and starlet who became Miss Army Recruiting of 1962.

"I don't think any actress expresses the complexities of her time and generation, its whole quest for fulfillment and an identity in society, as much as Jane," said Alan Pakula, who directed her Oscar-winning performance in *Klute*. Jane's life, often lived on the pages of newspapers and magazines, sometimes seems to have followed the same path as the baby boomers born only a few years later than she: They all struggled along with the rest of the nation to turn from war to fairness and peace.

There are certainly many qualities in Jane's life that are worthy of emulation. In that sense, what is important is not the specific stands she has taken but her effort to be true to herself and to have the courage to support her own vision, however it changes and wherever it leads. Jane's vision has included not only becoming successful in business but having a closely knit "traditional" family to cook for, worry over, come home to, and love. Visions and circumstances change over time; integrity, commitment, and courage are the constants that provide the driving force.

These days, Jane says she is "superaware" of her feelings, welcomes criticism and even seeks it out. "That's how I grow," she says. And if she makes a mistake, if she offends someone? "I will never try to justify myself. I will apologize and I will change." That makes her a lot more human than people may think. They don't expect her to be "just folks," but "I feel very much like ordinary people," she says. "I'm much more middle-of-the-road than people expect me to be. . . . I'm not some scary, awful, judgmental person."

Much of Jane's life has been based on the belief that you need to be informed about what you are doing and that you can make a difference. "I don't believe those who say in five years' time we'll pollute ourselves out of existence. That's a fatalistic attitude—a great copout for not doing anything."

There have been times when Jane's activism has interfered with her great natural gifts and sidetracked her from a career as an actress. But what she has learned from those experiences has deepened her ability to understand the characters she portrays. "An actress is supposed to reflect life," Jane says, "and the only way to do that is to participate in life. Life is not Hollywood."

Finding out who you are, what you believe, and even what to do with your life are not easy tasks. They are not accomplished in a day, and there is never a time when an answer is revealed forever so that you can sink back in contentment and become "soggy." There are always new opportunities, new challenges, and new questions as life unfolds.

"Many of us feel there is no purpose in life," Jane says, "and our society no longer seems able to provide an answer, a direction, for us. It seems to me, one purpose of life is to do everything we can to make things better."

AN INTERVIEW
WITH
JANE FONDA

For the readers of this book, Jane granted an extraordinary and
wide-ranging interview in which she discussed every aspect of
the story that has just been presented. Seated comfortably in the
small library of her attractive and unpretentious home in Santa
Monica, California, she spoke candidly about her childhood,
her careers, and her family. Many of those comments have
already been incorporated into the text, along with anecdotes
and details never before made public.

Part of the conversation, however, was specifically about
feelings and insights she wanted to share with the readers of this
book.

Q. What are your concerns about today's youth and your own
children? What do you most want to tell them?
A. One of the things I would want to tell my children and their
friends is: Don't let yourself give in to a feeling of hopeless-
ness and apathy. You have been handed a world that isn't
always pretty and that has a lot of problems. They're not
problems that you created, yet you have to bear the burden
of those problems. Just don't forget that you can make a
difference and that you can change things.

Individually, you can make a difference in your home, in your community, and in your own individual life by striving to be as good a person as you can and to make the most of your potential. In a broader sense, in the country and in the world, you can make a difference by joining with other people in opposing things you think are wrong and encouraging and promoting things you think are right.

If you don't like apartheid in South Africa, you should join with your friends in opposing it. If you're frightened about the notion of nuclear war, you should learn what it means and join with your friends and your parents or with other people in letting the government know how you feel. A big lesson for all of us in the sixties was that we could make a difference. I know you're not told that very often, and sometimes older people and even schoolbooks give the impression that the sixties "failed," that they never led to anything. But that's not true.

Many of us went through profound changes. We changed our lives. We changed our values. And we learned that if we were willing to stand up and voice our feelings and become active, we could change our government's policies. It took a lot longer than we anticipated in the beginning, but in the end we made our point. We won, and the war ended.

Q. That's talking politically. Do you notice that kids are politically concerned today?

A. Yes. That doesn't mean that all kids are politically concerned. That's too much of a generalization. But my experience is that children have vague impressions about Vietnam and vague impressions about the sixties, fears about nuclear war, and concerns about the environment. That may all seem like a gray, confused haze. But they are thinking about it more than people sometimes give them credit for—especially by the time they are in junior high and high school.

Q. Do you think kids today feel adults don't appreciate their joys and pleasures?

A. Every kid, always, throughout history, feels like, "Don't tell me this is always what you go through as an adolescent." Everyone feels this period of adolescence is something unique to them.

Q. I suppose those of us who grew up in the sixties are particularly guilty of thinking that we were special and that the times of our youth were special, too.

A. In the sixties, there was an excitement and a sense that we were changing the world. But there were other periods of upheaval and courage, inspiration and change and hope. It was a tremendous rude awakening for a lot of us, and there was no question that there was a sense that we could change the world. But I react strongly to the feeling that we peaked during the sixties and that it's all downhill from there.

Q. I agree that we made a lot of progress in the sixties. But racism, for example, is still a significant part of people's lives.

A. It would be a lie to say that racism has been abolished in this country. And I'm sure there are times when minority kids feel despair at the inequities in our society. But this is where it's important to learn about history. Change has always been a very slow, painful process.

But in the South, in the early sixties, which was not so long ago, blacks were not allowed to participate in our system. They were not allowed to vote. And they began to organize. They were not allowed to sit at lunch counters. They were not allowed to ride in the front of buses and had to sit in the back. There was institutionalized segregation.

They organized against it. They were joined by a certain number of white people, and segregation in the South was broken. Blacks got the right to vote. And that was not so long ago. The lesson from that is—don't sit back and accept racism as a fact of life. Speak out against it. Organize against it. Fight back against it. Don't take it sitting down.

Q. What would you tell young people about sex?
A. What I would say to young people about sex is that it's okay to say no. It's okay not to have sex whenever somebody else wants it. Your body belongs to you. And the only way sex can be really satisfying to you is when you have it with somebody that you're not frightened of and that you are attracted to and that you care for. That's when sex really has pleasure and meaning. Until you feel safe and loved and respected by somebody, why not keep yourself to yourself?

If you *are* going to have sex, use precautions for birth control and against AIDS. Use condoms.

Q. Do you think condoms should be available in the schools?
A. I do, absolutely. I think sex education and birth-control devices should be a part of education. Ideally, parents and the family should teach it to kids. But since that is not happening, then the schools should do it, in my opinion.

Q. And what would you say to young people about drugs and alcohol?
A. If I found that my children were using drugs, I would trot them down to Cedars-Sinai Hospital to the floor where there are teenage kids who have become vegetables and zombies because of overdosing on drugs. I would just show them what happens and try to scare the bejesus out of them.

I have said to my children, "I cannot police you at every moment when you are out of this house. I cannot control what you do when you are not in this house. But when you are in this house, there are no drugs. There is no alcohol. I am opposed to it. I think it will destroy your life. You are growing people, and you have to have clear minds in order to think clearly and make important decisions for yourselves."

Q. Do you mean, they cannot do drugs while they are living here?

A. I mean doing it under the roof. I cannot know what you do outside. But I want you to know that I disapprove of the use of drugs. And the only way I can demonstrate and enforce that is when you are under this roof. In our house *you* do not do it. I don't want you to do it anywhere, but there are some families who say, If you are going to do it, do it in front of me. I think that is the wrong signal to send to kids.

Q. Do you feel the same way about marijuana as you do about cocaine or needles?

A. Yes, I do. If you are looking for a high, you are looking for an excuse, an escape. It alters your mind. It affects your ability to think straight and to concentrate in class and to make good judgments. Obviously, marijuana is less dangerous to the body than cocaine or heroin, but it *is* something that gets in the way of growing up.

Q. What are your feelings about tobacco?

A. I think anyone who smokes cigarettes is a fool, just a fool. Anybody who cares knows today that the risks of cancer and heart disease are increased incredibly by smoking. If people go ahead and do it anyway, they're just crazy and they have no respect for themselves. It's disgusting to see young people smoking.

Q. Of course, the standard excuse for any of this behavior is "peer pressure."

A. That's what I meant in the beginning about sex. It's okay to say no. Smoking because of peer pressure or because you want to appear cool is stupidity. The person who is cool is the person who stands up to foolish peer pressure and does what is right for themselves. Any young person who is seen smoking just looks like a fool to anybody who knows anything.

Q. You used to smoke yourself, didn't you?

A. I stopped smoking twenty years ago as it became more and more clear how dangerous it was. I had friends who stopped who had smoked a lot more than I did. I never smoked all that much, anyway. And I said to myself, if they can stop— and they smoke more than I do—then I'm really going to make an effort.

    I suffered for about two weeks. Really suffered. It's sort of like going into war. You just have to say to yourself, I'm going into battle. I'm going to battle this demon, and I'm going to win, but I recognize that for a certain period of time it's warfare.

Q. Do you want to say something about bulimia here?

A. Yes. I started when I was seventeen. Like most bulimics, I started when I was a teenager. And it's a disease, like alcoholism or drug addiction. It's a very, very serious disease. It doesn't mean that you're a bad person, either. Some of the most disciplined and together people I know have suffered from bulimia. And in every other area of their lives, they're very together.

    There are a lot of differences of opinion about why someone starts and why it's so hard to stop. But it's very, very difficult to stop on your own. Anyone who has bulimia should not keep it a secret and should seek professional help. There is no one cure for everybody. For very extreme cases, hospitalization is recommended. There are drugs that are given to help some individuals. Hypnosis. Individual therapy. Overeaters Anonymous, which works on the same

Twelve Step program as Alcoholics Anonymous. All of these things—alone or in conjunction with each other—can help. Don't be a hero and try to do it on your own.

Q. One thing that impressed me in doing the research for this book is that much of your life has been very hard. You were hit very hard by the divorce of Brooke Hayward's parents, for example, and by your own parents' divorce. Today divorce is very casual, but it hasn't always been that way.

A. When our grandparents were married, for the most part they were married for life. It was a commitment. Now it's quite facile, and parents don't understand how terrifying it is for kids.

I know from our summer camp that there are solitary kids whose parents are not living together. It's just a nightmare. And they don't often talk about it. Once in a while, though, an entire camp will get together and talk about divorce. And they need to talk about it instead of thinking it's a perfectly natural thing and no big deal.

The way you cover it up is just the way I did, just the way my daughter does. "Well, they didn't get along and so, you know, gosh, I don't want them to live together because my mom and dad wouldn't get along." Bull! It's terrifying. Just terrifying.

Q. How did you come through the death of your mother and other people around you?

A. One thing I've learned over the years is that a particular tragedy can make one person stronger and destroy another. No one knows why. I have no idea why. Maybe, ultimately, these things have not made me stronger. But I've certainly survived and in some ways become stronger because of the hardships. Even within the same family, someone might come through and another might be totally undermined by the same incidents. Who knows?

Q. How do you feel about today's far-out trends in dressing and makeup—things like purple Mohawk haircuts?

A. I think it's fun. I think back to people's reactions to hippie styles that were so outrageous. Hey, I would much prefer to have my kids shave their head, have a purple Mohawk and a safety pin through their ear than to look perfectly normal and be shooting drugs. Do you know what I mean? It's just your exterior. It's just the way you look. You're quite right to feel rebellious. And if that's the way you're going to work out your form of rebellion, there's nothing wrong with it. It's when you start monkeying around with your head, with your insides, with drugs and alcohol, that it starts getting dangerous.

Q. If you could go back and talk to yourself as a teenager, give yourself a good shake and say, "Listen, you," what would you say to yourself? What do you wish you had known then that you do know now?

A. I would have stayed in school. I would have studied harder. I would have tried to really use those years in school instead of just getting by.

You know, if you don't have inspiring teachers, then it's really hard just being put through the system. But it's the only time in life that you have time to devote to learning and not to all the other stuff, the responsibilities you have when you grow up. I didn't take full advantage of it, and that I really regret.

Q. What does the future look like to you? What do you think the next fifty years are going to be like?

A. I'm basically an optimistic person, so I feel that the human will to survive and keep going as a species will prevail. But I think also that we as human beings determine our own future. That's why, for me, it's so important to keep encouraging people to take their own responsibility for the future. It's up to us what the future looks like. And I'm confident that we'll have the sense to make it a good future.

Q. Thank you very much.
A. It's been fun.

NOTES

Unattributed quotes from Jane Fonda are from the author's interview with her on April 7, 1987.

9 Then Hepburn asked her . . .: *Jane Fonda's Workout Book*, pp. 54–55.

11 "My only major influence . . ." Haddad-Garcia, p. 10.

11 "a national monument" ibid p. 21.

11 "How can you compete . . ." Guiles, p. 15.

12 "Shut up!" . . . *My Life*, p. 33.

12 "And if I ever heard . . ." Haddad-Garcia, p. 12.

12 "I was brought up . . ." Los Angeles Jewish Federation, "Fonda and Bradley Speak Out for Ethiopian Jewry," *The Bulletin*, Vol. 27, March 21, 1985, p. 14.

13 "My father wants . . ." Hedda Hopper, "Fonda, Vadim Enjoying View," *Los Angeles Times Calendar*, August 15, 1965.

13 "A great huzzah went up . . ." *My Life*, p. 24.

15 "It's not war . . ." Guiles, p. 12.

16 description of house: "Fonda's Formula for Successful Living," *House Beautiful*, Vol. 40, July 1948, p. 4. See also: Kiernan, pp. 21 and 27.

20 "I spent my childhood . . ." Kiernan, p. 18.

20 "Are you a boy . . ." Alfred Arnowitz, "Lady Jane," *Saturday Evening Post*, Vol. 236, March 23, 1963, p. 22.

21 "I loved him . . ." "The Cause Celeb," *Newsweek*, November 16, 1970, p. 65.

22 "lakes and swamps . . ." *My Life*, p. 186.

22 "When we left Tigertail . . ." "I hate the East" "It was a rotten summer . . ." "There was a big deal . . ." ibid, p. 185.

23 "He didn't buy them . . ." ibid, p. 187.
26 "I came home from school . . ." ibid, p. 203.
26 "I don't want you . . ." ibid.
26 "How weird . . . cry" ibid, p. 204.
26 "It's the only . . ." ibid, p. 205.
28 "a ravishing beauty," Kiernan, p. 54.
28 "Susan was everything . . ." *My Life*, p. 213.
28 "I'm not sure . . ." "Interview: Peter Fonda," *Playboy*, Vol. 17, September 1970, p. 85.
29 "Dear God, . . . anyhow." *My Life*, p. 215.
29 "Happy Birthday . . ." ibid, p. 216.
29 "incredibly charming" ibid, p. 219.
30 "I remember bingeing . . ." *Jane Fonda's Workout Book*, p. 13.
31 "My roommate believed . . ." ibid, p. 14.
31 "the disease has reached . . ." *Los Angeles Times*, December 27, 1984.
32 Yet that spring . . . open it.: Vadim, p. 238.
32 "Something about . . ." Kiernan, p. 58.
33 "Well, gosh, . . ." *Saturday Evening Post*, March 23, 1963.
33 "At rehearsals . . ." Kiernan, p. 58.
34 "It wasn't anything . . ." *My Life*, p. 239.
34 "Yes, I've known . . ." ibid, p. 242.
35 "I did nothing . . ." Kiernan, p. 64.
35 "totally unpredictable . . ." *My Life*, p. 246.
35 "Everyone . . . forget it!" Kiernan, p. 65.
36 "until I realized . . ." *Jane Fonda's Workout Book*, p. 15.
36 "When she came on . . ." *Life*, February 22, 1960.
37 "But of course . . ." ibid.
37 The last time that . . .: *My Life*, p. 252.
37 "with that wonderful . . ." Dick Williams, "Jane Fonda's Own Answer to Questions," *Los Angeles Times Calendar*, November 26, 1962.
37 "By then . . ." Kiernan, p. 71.
37 "I was brought up . . ." Edwin Miller, "Fervent Eyes of Fonda Blue," *Seventeen*, September 1972, p. 134.
37 "He was so guarded . . ." Adfera Fonda, p. 9.
38 "Jane was almost . . ." ibid, p. 37.
38 Peter was best man . . .: *My Life*, p. 254.
38 "I've always been ashamed . . ." "Jane Fonda at Forty," *Family Weekly*, March 12, 1978, p. 6.
39 "It was the craziest . . ." *My Life*, p. 258.
39 "I was very friendly . . ." Guiles, p. 44.
40 "young ladies were . . ." Kiernan, p. 75.
41 "I went to Paris . . ." ibid.

41 "I was frightened . . ." "Three Faces of Fonda," *Show Business Illustrated,* November 28, 1961, p. 46.

41 "Underneath everything . . ." Kiernan, p. 80.

42 "Why aren't you . . . something to do." *Saturday Evening Post,* op. cit.

43 "The only reason . . ." *Life,* op cit.

43 "On top of that . . . which it did." John G. Houser, "Volatile Jane Fonda," *Los Angeles Herald Examiner,* March 23, 1964.

45 looking so confused . . .: *My Life,* p. 265.

45 "major, *major* self-doubt . . ." Ron Rosenbaum, "Dangerous Jane," *Vanity Fair,* November 1988.

45 "plain Jane," Kiernan, p. 109.

46 "There's no question . . ." *Saturday Evening Post.* op. cit.

46 "Jane has made . . ." Kiernan, p. 110.

48 "Kitty Twist . . ." Hedda Hopper gossip column, *Los Angeles Times Calendar,* July 9, 1961, p. 3.

48 "It took place . . ." ibid.

48 "I really love it . . ." ibid.

48 "I think the only thing . . ." *Saturday Evening Post,* op cit.

49 "I think marriage . . ." Hedda Hopper gossip column, *Chicago Sunday Times Magazine,* July 9, 1961.

49 "After all, . . ." *Saturday Evening Post,* op cit.

49 Jane felt that her whole childhood . . .: Hedda Hopper, "Jane Fonda Mellows on Young Ideas," *Los Angeles Times Calendar,* July 8, 1962.

49 "Somehow making movies . . ." Haddad-Garcia, p. 62.

50 "Even the sight . . ." Richard Watts, *New York Post,* October 27, 1962.

50 "What will become . . ." Stanley Kauffman, *The New Republic,* February 1964.

52 "I discovered . . ." Freedland, p. 167.

52 "about as devilish . . ." Donald R. Katz, "Jane Fonda, A Hard Act to Follow," *Rolling Stone,* March 9, 1978, p. 39.

52 "Nothing is more . . ." Freedland, p. 167.

53 "Then it don't matter . . ." *My Life,* p. 131.

54 "I think it's the most . . . perfect movie." Freedland, p. 78.

54 "courageous, but tender . . ." Vadim, *Bardot Deneuve Fonda,* p. 236.

55 "This Frenchman . . ." Doris Klein, "Parisian Influence Strong on Jane," *Los Angeles Times,* December 2, 1964.

56 "He will not settle . . ." *Los Angeles Times,* August 15, 1965.

56 "I love Vadim . . ." Kiernan, p. 174.

57 kept in touch . . . each day: Freedland, p. 94.

57 "I think honesty . . ." Kiernan, p. 182.

57 "superficial but very pleasant" Vadim, op cit., p. 238.

63 "niggers gettin' the best . . ." Haddad-Garcia, p. 133.

63 "We had this swimming . . ." ibid, p. 134.

63 "So thick you could . . ." "You never saw . . ." Kiernan, p. 199.

63 Charmed, she bent down . . .: Vadim, op cit., p. 162.

65 "It became necessary . . ." W. Rademaekers, "Growing Fonda Jane," *Time*, Vol. 110, October 3, 1977, p. 90.

66 "Everybody will be waiting . . ." Haddad-Garcia, p. 143.

67 he dutifully went back . . .: Joyce Haber, "More to Jane Fonda Than Meets the Eye," *Los Angeles Times Calendar*, January 19, 1969.

67 During the 1970s, . . .: Mary Blume, "Jane Fonda an Optimist of the Soul," *Los Angeles Times Calendar*, February 20, 1972.

67 "a certain charm . . ." *Jane Fonda's Workout Book*, p. 18.

68 "My eyes were opened . . . obviously . . . good job." Freedland, pp. 139–140.

70 "a savage, decisive blow," National Security Council member Roger Morris in Hersh, p. 127.

70 "Those Americans who . . ." ibid, p. 130.

71 twenty-nine days before the alert was canceled.: Hersh, p. 124.

71 "What a nice gesture . . ." Haddad-Garcia, p. 46.

71 "I had never felt . . ." Kiernan, p. 223.

73 "Before long . . ." Kiernan, p. 235.

74 "Who am I? . . ." *L.A. Weekly*, November 28, 1980.

76 "I'd grown up . . ." Haddad-Garcia, p. 51.

79 "my alleged daughter" *Newsweek*, November 16, 1970, op. cit.

79 "We're very close . . ." Kiernan, p. 225.

80 On Hoover's attempts to malign Jane's character, see "Phony FBI Letter to Smear Jane Fonda Disclosed," Robert Rawitch, *Los Angeles Times*, December 16, 1975; and "Hoover Authorized Attempt at Tricking DV Into Running Phony Item," *Daily Variety*, December 18, 1975.

81 "I'm not a do-gooder . . ." Martin Kasindorf, "Fonda, A Person of Many Parts," *New York Times Magazine*, February 3, 1974, p. 16.

81 "complexes about my . . ." "Plenty of people . . ." "Well, I made . . ." Kiernan, p. 233.

83 "I don't think . . ." *Los Angeles Herald Examiner*, February 9, 1984.

84 "In the process . . ." ibid.

85 "I implore you . . ." Kiernan, p. 281.

85 "There's a lot I . . ." Guiles, p. 187.

86 "Because she was . . ." *My Life*, p. 310.

86 "I'm not unhappy . . ." Guiles, p. 184.

87 Jane filed suit . . .: Myrna Oliver, "Victory in Privacy Suit Claimed by Jane Fonda," *Los Angeles Times*, May 8, 1979.

90 "I don't have . . ." Kovic, *Born on the Fourth of July*, p. 141.

91 Obie citation: *Village Voice*, May 11, 1972.

92 "Your heart speeding up . . ." Kiernan, p. 275.

92 "I was very cynical . . ." "Interview: Jane Fonda and Tom Hayden," *Playboy*, Vol. 21, April 1974, p. 67.

92 "single greatest figure . . ." Paul Berman, "At the Center of the 60's" (review of *Reunion*), *The New York Times*, June 12, 1988.

92 "society should be organized . . ." *Playboy*, April 1974, op cit.

93 "a very funny man": P. C. McAuley, "Fonda, Hayden, Bonded, Balanced by Yin/Yang," *Los Angeles Times*, February 19, 1984.

93 "funny looking . . ." *L.A. Weekly*, November 28, 1980.

93 "Who are you . . . nobody" *Playboy*, April 1972, op cit.

95 "We were holding hands . . ." David Gritten, "Political Bedfellows," *People*, Vol. 17, May 24, 1982, p. 38.

95 "She had an intensity . . ." *L.A. Weekly*, November 28, 1980.

97 "I didn't go . . ." *Playboy*, April 1972, op cit.

97 "When you're famous . . ." Erica Jong, "Jane Fonda: An Interview," *Ladies Home Journal*, Vol. 101, April 1984, p. 32.

99 "Do you think . . ." Haddad-Garcia, p. 62.

99 "she spread . . ." *Los Angeles Herald Examiner*, June 14, 1973.

99 "If Congress wants . . ." *Daily Variety*, September 8, 1973.

100 "It was a grueling . . ." Kiernan, p. 285.

101 splashed Jane in the face . . .: *Newsweek*, April 16, 1973.

102 "Peter and Jane . . . obscene." *My Life*, pp. 301 and 302.

103 "It would be foolish . . ." *Daily Variety*, September 7, 1973.

103 "tens of thousands . . ." *Los Angeles Times*, June 9, 1973.

104 students hanged her in effigy.: Lee Harris, "Jane Fonda Hanged in Effigy at Her USC Talk," *Los Angeles Times*, April 13, 1973.

104 "for the rottenest . . ." remark by Rep. Robert Steele (Rep.-CT), *Los Angeles Herald Examiner*, April 3, 1973.

104 "Quite frankly . . ." remark by Kirby Holmes in *New Times*, November 16, 1979.

104 "Why did Nixon . . ." "I'm very weary . . ." *Playboy*, April 1972, op cit.

106 "that shack": Cole, p. 153.

106 "no yard . . ." Joan Goodman, "Jane Fonda in Charge," *Elle*, December 1986. Also see photos: Stacy Peck, "Jane Fonda and Tom Hayden," *Los Angeles Times Home Magazine*, December 6, 1981, p. 62.

107 On *Introduction to the Enemy*, see Jane Fonda, "A Vietnam Journal— Rebirth of a Nation," *Rolling Stone*, July 4, 1974.

107 "I ate and dressed . . ." *Playboy*, April 1972, op cit.

107 "The most important thing . . ." Kiernan, p. 271.

107 "A lot of people thought . . ." John M. Wilson, "Jane Fonda's Happy Heist," *The New York Times*, April 11, 1976.

107 "She was thinking . . ." Phyllis Batelle, "The Unknown Jane Fonda," *Ladies Home Journal*, Vol. 102, October 1985, p. 42.

108 "The radicalism . . ." Richard Kelly, "Interview: Jane Fonda," *The Advocate,* June 2, 1976.

111 "KGB . . ." Robert Gillette, "Refusenik Tells Plight to Fonda on Soviet Soil," *Los Angeles Times,* March 2, 1984.

112 "Running . . ." "If you don't . . ." ibid.

112 "I can't tell you what . . ." Freedland, p. 239.

112 "Once you say . . ." Patricia Ward, "Fonda Crosses Lines in Efforts for Soviet Jews," *Los Angeles Times,* March 15, 1985.

113 "Nobody ever asked . . ." *Los Angeles Times,* March 15, 1985.

113 "Oh, just to be able . . ." Jack Kroll, "Hollywood's New Heroines," *Newsweek,* October 10, 1977.

113 "It's the first time . . ." Margaret Drabble, "Jane Fonda: Her Own Woman at Last?" *Ms,* October 1977.

113 visit Lillian Hellman: Charles Higham, "Jane Fonda at 40," *US,* November 1, 1977.

114 "Have you ever . . . it works." Guiles, p. 247.

115 "a very important film" Haddad-Garcia, p. 205.

116 "It's possible to say . . ." *The Advocate,* op cit.

116 "fairly traditional" *Los Angeles Herald Examiner,* January 21, 1980.

116 "The more you . . ." *Los Angeles Times Calendar,* April 29, 1984.

116 "Very often . . ." *People,* May 24, 1982, op cit.

118 "I consider myself . . ." Guiles, p. 262.

118 state arts council.: Jerry Gillam, "Senate Rejects Jane Fonda for Arts Council," *Los Angeles Times,* July 21, 1979; Jerry Gillam and W. B. Rood, "Brown Calls Rejection of Miss Fonda Gutless Act," *Los Angeles Times,* July 28, 1979.

118 "Those were rough . . ." *People,* May 24, 1982, op cit.

118 "there's a certain . . ." *Los Angeles Times Calendar,* April 29, 1984.

118 "One category . . ." *Ladies Home Journal,* October 1985, op cit.

119 For further firsthand research, . . .: Marua Moynihan and Andy Warhol, "Jane Fonda," *Interview,* March 1984.

120 "I'm not a religious man . . ." *My Life,* p. 349.

121 "Well, it's about time," ibid, p. 344.

121 "They were playing out . . ." Adfera Fonda, p. 170.

122 "Don't worry, . . ." Lois Armstrong, "For Jane, Those Days 'On Golden Pond' Brought Her and Her Dad Together," *People,* Vol. 17, April 12, 1982, p. 28.

123 "How can we live . . ." Celeste Fremon, "Checking in with The First Lady of Fitness and Film," *Playgirl,* October 1985, p. 147.

123 "If only . . ." "not a rehearsal" *Whole Life Times,* November–December 1984.

123 "It was a strange . . ." *Playgirl,* op cit.

123 "And what I realized . . . might lose them." ibid.

124 "I rebelled . . ." Interview in *Whole Life Times*, March 1984.

126 "It was the first . . ." *Jane Fonda's Workout Book.*

126 "Not to anyone. . . ." *Playgirl*, op cit.

127 "Bulimia is an illness . . . weak or bad person" *Jane Fonda's New Workout and Weight Loss Program*, p. 17.

127 "It is usually advisable . . ." ibid, p. 19.

127 "Tell the people . . ." ibid, p. 20.

127 "People who want . . ." ibid.

128 "I found that when . . ." *USA Today*, May 22, 1985.

128 "I think that when . . . someone else." *L.A. Weekly*, November 28, 1980.

129 "it would have meant . . ." *Playgirl*, op cit.

129 "This district . . ." *People*, May 24, 1982, op cit.

129 She spent four hours . . .: Robert W. Stewart, "Fonda Takes Her Act On the Road to Aid Hayden's Drive," *Los Angeles Times*, May 3, 1982.

130 "My refrigerator . . ." Sidney Skolsky, "Jane Fonda Panic Girl," *Hollywood Citizen-News*, August 3, 1961.

131 "As it began . . . still an actress." Richard Stayton, "Is Jane Fonda Slowing Down?" *Los Angeles Herald Examiner*, May 13, 1984.

132 "Most of the women . . ." *Whole Life Times*, November 12, 1984.

133 "What does a smallmouth . . ." *People*, January 18, 1980.

133 "I just wanted . . ." *San Francisco Examiner*, August 28, 1964.

133 "My only regret . . ." *Ladies Home Journal*, October 1985, op cit.

134 "You don't look . . ." *Whole Life Times*, op cit.

134 "I wouldn't want . . . I don't think I'm unique." ibid.

134 "What's bad about aging? . . ." *USA Today*, May 22, 1985.

135 "When she first came . . ." *Whole Life Times*, op cit.

135 "To have a house . . ." *Ladies Home Journal*, April 1984, op cit.

135 "When you're married . . ." *L.A. Weekly*, November 28, 1980.

136 "Like most marriages . . ." *Los Angeles Times*, February 19, 1984.

137 "If Jane and I . . ." John Balzar, "Hayden, Fonda Separate," *Los Angeles Times*, February 16, 1989.

138 "As a child . . ." *Jane Fonda's Workout Book*, p. 13.

138 "The glow and energy . . ." ibid, p. 16.

139 "It worries me . . ." Loren MacArthur, "In Her Prime," *City Sports Magazine*, March 1986.

139 "The polls say . . ." ibid.

140 "You can't ignore . . ." *Los Angeles Times Calendar*, April 29, 1984.

141 "the most challenging . . ." ibid.

141 "a mountain woman . . ." George Haddad-Garcia, "My Side," *Working Women*, April 1984.

141 "Look, there have been . . ." *Los Angeles Herald Examiner*, May 13, 1984.

141 "I entered a world . . ." ibid.

142 "I especially learned . . ." *The New York Times*, May 13, 1984.

142 "Lucy is an artist . . ." *Ladies Home Journal*, April 1984, op cit.

143 "I'm here . . ." "somebody trying . . ." "She's like so many, . . ." *Los Angeles Times Calendar*, April 29, 1984.

143 "Over the years . . ." *Los Angeles Herald Examiner*, May 13, 1984.

144 "Well, Miss Fonda . . ." *The New York Times*, May 13, 1984.

144 "It was the hardest . . ." *Los Angeles Times Calendar*, April 29, 1984.

145 "I have always . . ." *Vanity Fair*, November 1988.

145 "I believe in a . . ." Julia Cameron, "Jane Fonda Is Right Where She Wants To Be," *Chicago Tribune*, September 8, 1985.

145 "a redneck . . ." *Movieline*, August 8, 1986.

145 "an explosion . . ." ibid.

146 "I met Carlos . . ." Gregg Barrios, " 'Old Gringo': Romance, Revolution, Sex, Passion," *Los Angeles Times Calendar*, April 24, 1988.

146 "When Harriet Arrives . . ." ibid.

147 "This isn't an easy . . ." ibid.

148 spit at a priest . . .: Jack Goldberg, "Board Soundly Rejects Anti-Fonda Resolution," *Waterbury American*, April 25, 1988.

148 "And yet . . ." Randall Beach, "Vets' Real Enemy Within Themselves; It's Not Jane Fonda," *New Haven Register*, April 25, 1988.

149 Agent Orange benefit. "Jane Fonda Finds Peace in Her Time," *The New York Times*, August 4, 1988; "Fonda Undeterred by N.E. Protests," *Hollywood Register*, August 5, 1988.

149 Later that month . . . "Nose for News," *Los Angeles Herald Examiner*, October 16, 1988; *Hollywood Reporter*, October 13, 1988.

150 "One of the great things . . ." *The New York Times Magazine*, February 3, 1974.

151 "I don't think any . . ." ibid.

151 "That's how I grow . . ." *Ladies Home Journal*, October 1985, op cit.

151 "I feel very much . . ." *Los Angeles Times*, February 19, 1984.

151 "I don't believe . . ." *Seventeen*, September 1972, op cit.

152 "An actress is supposed . . ." *The New York Times Magazine*, February 3, 1974.

152 "Many of us feel . . ." *Women's Wear Daily*, October 28, 1974.

BIBLIOGRAPHY

Cole, Gerald and Wes Farrell. *The Fondas*. New York: St. Martin's Press, 1984.

Fincer, Ernest Barksdale. *The Vietnam War*. New York: Franklin Watts, 1980.

Fonda, Afdera. *Never Before Noon*. New York: Weidenfeld & Nicholson, 1987.

Fonda, Henry. *Fonda, My Life* (as told to Howard Teichmann). New York: New American Library, 1981.

Fonda, Jane. *Jane Fonda's Workout Book*. New York: Simon & Schuster, 1981.

Fonda, Jane and Mignon McCarthy. *Women Coming of Age*. New York: Simon & Schuster, 1984.

Freedland, Michael. *Jane Fonda*. New York: St. Martin's Press, 1988.

Guiles, Fred Lawrence. *Jane Fonda, The Actress in Her Time*. New York: Doubleday, 1982.

Haddad-Garcia, George. *The Films of Jane Fonda*. Secaucus, N.J.: The Citadel Press, 1981.

Hayden, Tom. *Trial*. Orlando, Fla.: Holt, Rinehart and Winston, 1970.

Hayden, Tom. *Reunion*. New York: Random House, 1988.

Hersh, Seymour M. *The Prince of Power: Kissinger in the Nixon White House*. New York: Summit Books, 1983.

Kiernan, Thomas. *Jane, An Intimate Biography*. N.Y.: G. P. Putnam's Sons, 1973.

Kovic, Ron. *Born on the Fourth of July*. New York: McGraw-Hill, 1976.

Spada, James. *Fonda, Her Life in Pictures*. New York: Doubleday, 1985.

Vadim, Roger. *Memoirs of the Devil*. San Diego: Harcourt Brace Jovanovich, 1977.

Vadim, Roger. *Bardot Deneuve Fonda*. New York: Simon & Schuster, 1986.

INDEX